The Multiliteracies Classroom

NEW PERSPECTIVES ON LANGUAGE AND EDUCATION
Series Editor: Professor Viv Edwards, University of Reading, Reading, Great Britain
Series Advisor: Professor Allan Luke, Queensland University of Technology, Brisbane, Australia

Two decades of research and development in language and literacy education have yielded a broad, multidisciplinary focus. Yet education systems face constant economic and technological change, with attendant issues of identity and power, community and culture. This series will feature critical and interpretive, disciplinary and multidisciplinary perspectives on teaching and learning, language and literacy in new times.

Full details of all the books in this series and of all our other publications can be found on http://www.multilingual-matters.com, or by writing to Multilingual Matters, St Nicholas House, 31–34 High Street, Bristol BS1 2AW, UK.

NEW PERSPECTIVES ON LANGUAGE AND EDUCATION
Series Editor: Professor Viv Edwards, University of Reading,
Reading, Great Britain

The Multiliteracies Classroom

Kathy A. Mills

MULTILINGUAL MATTERS
Bristol • Buffalo • Toronto

*This book is dedicated to Lachlan Henry
and Juliette Elizabeth Mills.*

Library of Congress Cataloging in Publication Data
A catalog record for this book is available from the Library of Congress.
Mills, Kathy, 1974–
The Multiliteracies Classroom/Kathy A. Mills.
Includes bibliographical references and index.
1.   Literacy--Study and teaching. 2.   Literacy--Study and teaching--Australia.
3.   Interactive multimedia.
I. Title.
LC149.M555 2010
418.007'dc22 2010041374

British Library Cataloguing in Publication Data
A catalogue entry for this book is available from the British Library.

ISBN-13: 978-1-84769-319-8 (hbk)
ISBN-13: 978-1-84769-318-1 (pbk)

Multilingual Matters
UK: St Nicholas House, 31–34 High Street, Bristol, BS1 2AW, UK.
USA: UTP, 2250 Military Road, Tonawanda, NY 14150, USA.
Canada: UTP, 5201 Dufferin Street, North York, Ontario, M3H 5T8, Canada.

The policy of Multilingual Matters/Channel View Publications is to use papers
that are natural, renewable and recyclable products, made from wood grown in
sustainable forests. In the manufacturing process of our books, and to further
support our policy, preference is given to printers that have FSC and PEFC Chain
of Custody certification. The FSC and/or PEFC logos will appear on those books
where full certification has been granted to the printer concerned.

Typeset by Techset Composition Ltd., Salisbury, UK.
Printed and bound in Great Britain by Short Run Press Ltd.

Contents

List of Tables

Acknowledgements

I was encouraged by two eminent professors to write this monograph – Allan Luke from Queensland University of Technology, and Phil Carspecken from Indiana University. Allan's internationally acclaimed work in critical sociology and literacy education has influenced my scholarship, and his advice has been invaluable at the most important junctures in my academic journey. Phil's internationally received publications in critical ethnography, and his critical ethnographic workshops have shaped my theoretical and methodological approach to this work.

Bill Cope and Mary Kalantzis, from the University of Illinois, are the driving force behind the original multiliteracies consensus. I thank them for contributing the foreword of this book, and for their professional support. Bill and Mary are visionaries of education in the new times.

I appreciate the critical contributions of Anna Healy and William Corcoran to the earlier formulations of this work. I give special thanks to 'Jennifer' (a pseudonym), the teacher participant whose classroom features in this research – this monograph would not have been possible without her generous participation.

I wish to thank my husband, Ryan, who did everything in his power to support the original research and writing of this book. His mother, Robyn, also gave very valuable assistance. Finally, I thank my parents, Henry and Marie Seltenrych, who made many sacrifices to provide me with every opportunity in education and in life.

Foreword

Jennifer teaches an upper primary class in a school located in a socio-economically disadvantaged suburban neighbourhood. This book tells her professional story, and the story of the 23 children with whom she works. These students have been streamed into her class because, according to the results they have achieved in a standardised literacy test, they are of 'low ability'.

Here, we meet Daria, the girl whose family came from the Sudan as refugees when she was four and who aspires to be a fashion model. We meet Ted, an Indigenous Australian boy, full of clever antics but with no books or computer at home. We meet Meliame, the girl who had migrated from Tonga a year ago and who now lives with her uncle and aunt because her father had to return home. And we meet Joshua, the white working class boy who dreams to work at McDonald's because there, he says, you can earn a lot of money.

This is a classroom full of energy and life, not just because the children are full of fun and hope, but also because of Jennifer's endlessly imaginative understanding of literacy. Soon she has her students enthusiastically creating digital animations, movies and web pages. She has them making exciting connections between real-world digital technologies and cutting-edge communications tasks.

The children's activities are never busywork. They also represent the contours of a challenging intellectual journey. The narrative of Jennifer's working life and her students' learning lives is a journey into the micro-dynamics of pedagogy. We witness students weaving between immersive experiences, abstract conceptualisation, critical analysis and real-world application. We see how Jennifer engages every fibre of their subjectivities, and cajoles or inspires them into higher-order thinking. We also see how she draws out and uses to brilliant effect the cadences of diversity among her children.

Jennifer, we come to realise, is an exceptional teacher. These children are very lucky to be in her class. But the story cannot be allowed to end there, and with the publication of this book, we know it will not.

As Jennifer, Daria, Ted, Meliame and Joshua and the rest of their class spring to life, we come to realise that this book does not just speak to the experience of a single teacher and 23 students. The narrative also tells the reader that what Jennifer has done could be done again and again, by any teacher anywhere, in this or their own way. Jennifer is an exceptional teacher, but her practices speak to all teachers. Every teacher can be exceptional. By describing Jennifer's repertoire of riskily imaginative practices and analysing her close attention to pedagogy, this book tells its readers, in vivid detail, how exceptional teaching can be done. It is this simple as well as this hard.

The Multiliteracies Classroom demonstrates in convincing detail how powerful learning can be achieved. Along the way, the book seamlessly weaves cutting-edge theoretical ideas into the fabric of its narrative. In one minute, we are hearing the teacher and students talking about rubbish in a pond or the case of the disappearing pimples. In the next, we hear what this means in the conceptualizations of Bakhtin or Vygotsky, of Bourdieu or Kress, of Gee or Cazden. In one moment, we hear the lilt of the accents of the children's discussions. In another, this is connected to the theoretical intricacies of 'discourse', 'heteroglossia', 'multimodality' or 'dialogic spaces'.

Kathy Mills has produced a masterpiece of qualitative research. The challenges, setbacks and problematic nuances of Jennifer's teaching are all there to be seen – this is not an uncritically laudatory account. However, we also witness the triumphs of a teacher who, in Mills' words, 'did not regard literacy as an independent variable. Rather, she regarded it as inseparable from social practices, contextualised in certain political, economic, historic and ecological contexts.'

Mary Kalantzis and Bill Cope
Champaign, Illinois, May 2010

Introduction

As a literacy educator, there are several influences that have helped to shape my thinking about the teaching of language and literacy in the 21st century. The first is multiliteracies. The second is critical sociology. The third is a sociocultural view of literacy, also known as the New Literacy Studies. I address multiliteracies in the classroom as social practice, endeavouring to understand how power works in the multiliteracies classroom, and the way this is tied up with patterns of power in the wider society.

This book will continue the revolutionary project of multiliteracies begun by the New London Group (1996), a group of 10 educators[1] who met together in New London, New Hampshire, to envisage new directions for literacy teaching and learning for the 21st century. The term 'multiliteracies' was coined by the New London Group to describe two arguments that convinced me of the need to extend the scope of literacy teaching. They argued that literacy teaching should be more responsive to the diversity of cultures, including subcultures, such as communities and affiliations, and the variety of languages within societies.

They also saw the need for literacy teaching to take into account the increasing range of text forms that are associated with information and multimedia technologies. A feature of the new media is multimodality – the interrelationship between two or more modes. The New London Group explained that the broadened range of texts is partially attributed to the diversity of cultures and subcultures (Cope & Kalantzis, 2000c).

Preferences in modes of representation, such as linguistic, auditory and gestural, differ according to culture and context, and have specific cognitive, social and relational effects. For example, in Aboriginal cultures the visual mode of representation is much richer and more evocative than linguistics alone (New London Group, 2000). Gestural modes of communication, represented through dance and holistic expressions of movement, are an integral part of Sudanese culture.

The book accomplishes three things: First, it recounts the complexities, challenges and rewards of engaging different students into new forms of communication with digital technologies; second, it demonstrates how new literacy pedagogies must take into account how power works in the classroom and the broader society; and third, it inspires readers to consider new possibilities for expanding literacy practices in the classroom to better prepare students for their life work in increasingly digitalised and multicultural societies.

Extending the work begun by the New London Group in multiliteracies, this book is relevant to those who have a stake in education around the globe: Students, teachers, principals, parents, teacher educators, researchers, policy makers, curriculum developers and governments. Readers can envisage how pioneering teachers negotiate the gradual digitalisation of print in classroom, schools and society. They can see cultural and linguistic diversity as a valuable resource for engaging students in new digital media, not just as consumers, but also as critical and creative producers. More importantly, at the heart of the book are important principles for understanding life and society beyond classrooms.

Chapter 1 Multiliteracies Matters describes the multiliteracies classroom, the teacher and the students, situating this within the local and global context. The chapter foregrounds the need to rethink literacy teaching to include new multimodal, digital and culturally inclusive practices for changing times.

Chapter 2 Situated and Explicit Pedagogy and Chapter 3 Critical and Creative Pedagogy analyse a series of media-based lessons in which students collaboratively design digital, animated movies. The inside story of the teacher's application of the multiliteracies pedagogy and Learning by Design is shared using classroom anecdotes of student learning. This narrative highlights the significant potentials and constraints that can be encountered when the multiliteracies pedagogy is implemented in multicultural and low-socioeconomic contexts.

Chapter 4 Multimodality, Media and Access investigates – rather than assumes – the potentials of multimodal literacies and new digital media to provide greater access to literacy learning in the multiliteracies classroom.

Chapter 5 New Social Spaces advances the currently underexplored yet fascinating social production of spaces – dialogic, bodily, embodied, architectonic and screen spaces – when new technologies for media production are integrated into the multiliteracies classroom.

Chapter 6 Discourses and Diversity uncovers the subconscious ways in which discourses – socially accepted ways of displaying membership in particular social groups through words, actions and other representations of self – can constrain or enable certain groups in the multiliteracies classroom.

Chapter 7 Power and Access gives valuable insights into the complex workings of power in the multiliteracies classroom, situating classroom events within patterns of power in the school, local community and society. The weighty consequences of ignoring issues of power in schools are revealed, making this chapter essential reading for all educators.

Chapter 8 New Times provides the inside perspectives of the multiliteracies teacher and culturally diverse students within her classroom. This chapter provides the outline of a social theory for understanding the distribution of multiliteracies in schools and society.

The work of theorising multiliteracies has already begun by a great many minds, stimulating an international uptake of new pedagogies for changing economic times. I am humbly appreciative of this work that paved the way for this research monograph. *The Multiliteracies Classroom* aims to do something very different to the existing literature on the topic. I endeavour to provide an accessible, first-hand account of the implementation of multiliteracies in mainstream and multicultural classrooms.

This book shows how teachers are negotiating principles and practices of multiliteracies in local contexts of diversity, interpreting these events in relation to underlying themes and values of critical theory that have resonated throughout the history of schooling. Extending ethnographic classroom research in a local context to principles of life and learning in an imperfect world, this book is intended to make a significant contribution to education for years to come.

Note

1. Original members of the New London Group who met in September 1994 and authored A Pedagogy of Multiliteracies in the *Harvard Educational Review* (1996) include Courtney B. Cazden, Bill Cope, Norman Fairclough, James Paul Gee, Mary Kalantzis, Gunther Kress, Allan and Carmen Luke, Sarah Michaels and Martin Nakata.

Chapter 1
Multiliteracies Matters

Researcher:	So tell me what your movie storyline is.
Jack¹:	'Slip, Slop, Slap!'
Nick:	Yeah.
Jack:	A man like, gets like, burned.
Nick:	Sunburnt.
Jack:	And he's, like, just got pants on. [No shirt for sun protection] And he's, he's, like, angry. Then he goes into the water, 'cause he thinks it's gunna make it better. But it gets worse. Then he gets angry.
Matthew:	Instead [interrupted].
Jack:	And then a lifeboat comes up with some sunscreen.
Matthew:	Instead of [interrupted].
Jack:	And then they all do a dance.
Matthew:	Instead of a lifeboat coming up with the sunscreen, why don't we have a big bottle of sunscreen pop up? [He gestures with hands to show figure popping onto the stage from below.]
Mark:	We need some sunscreen on it.
Jack:	Yeah! How about we make a big bottle of sunscreen and then it walks up to him!
Matthew:	Yeah! And it says, 'I'm sunscreen', and pours sunscreen all over him.

These four boys (aged 11–12 years) were collaboratively planning the storyboard or sequence of frames for their animated, digital movie. The movie had an authentic purpose, designed to communicate an educational message to the local school community, and to children in the lower primary grades.

The scenes in the final movie included generic representations of natural recreational sites, such as beaches and coral reef. The Gold and Sunshine

Coast, and the Great Barrier Reef, stretch for 2600 km along the Eastern coast of Queensland, the State where the boys live. These places of significance to the boys also play a key role in the tourist-driven economy of regional and metropolitan Queensland. In the vignette above, the boys made an intertextual reference to a famous Australian television health campaign for sun protection entitled 'Slip, Slop, Slap', which originally depicted an animated seagull with a lisp, who teaches viewers to 'Slip on a shirt, slop on sunscreen, and slap on a hat'.

Multiliteracies and Society

Interactions such as these demonstrate important shifts in literacy pedagogy and learning that are tied to broader shifts in the society in which these boys participate. The task of digital movie making required the boys to engage in authentic social practices of communication that are central to a globalised economy, using new technological tools of production, such as digital cameras, and movie editing and distribution software. Designing movies also requires proficiencies with dynamic combinations of modes, such as images, spatial arrangements, music, scripted voice-overs, gestures and animations, which include, but are not limited to, the encoded word (Mills, 2010b).

Historically, schools have emphasised teachers as experts, learners as novices and learning as the reproduction of disciplinary knowledge and decontextualised skills. What is observed here is a significant pedagogical shift, in which students are positioned to think and design collaboratively and creatively within a community of practice. The production of new media-based texts draws upon the collective, specialist and transdisciplinary expertise in open-ended engagements with new media design. This is the nature of new workplaces.

The pace of technological change in contemporary society means that digitally mediated textual practices are critical in a significant number of professions. Likewise, many workplaces emphasise change, flexibility, teamwork and networking rather than hierarchical command structures, deskilled work and mass production (Gee, 1994, 2000). Multi-skilled professionals, who have a broad portfolio of skills, and who engage in a dynamic repertoire of integrated practices, have replaced the division of labour into deskilled components (Cope & Kalantzis, 1999).

The theories presented in this book find their empirical basis in critical ethnographic research, conducted in intensive blocks of fieldwork over a three-year period. The narrative centres on the lives of an Australian teacher and her students in a suburban public school in a low-socioeconomic area. This historical account occurs at a time when these students will enter a globalised labour market. They will have to negotiate a broadening range of meaning-making systems, including online and other multimedia communication environments (New London Group, 2000).

The existing and emerging social practices in which these students must engage include reading books, resisting advertisements, using machines (scanners, printers, voicemail), interpreting public transport information, writing memos, following directories and maps and conducting internet transactions. Similarly, SMS messaging, word processing, emailing, internet relay chatting, internet navigation, critiquing websites, digital photography, slide-show presentations, computer programming and website design represent some of the diverse forms of literacy.

Using spreadsheets and databases, drama and vocal performance, film and media, image design, body language interpretation and oral debating are just a few among a plethora of communication practices used for a multiplicity of purposes in society today. The teacher in this study utilised new approaches to pedagogy to account for the increase of emergent text forms associated with information and multimedia technologies (Kalantzis *et al.*, 2002).

Australian Snapshot

The recent history of public schooling in Australia has seen a falling proportion of the gross domestic product (GDP) spent on the public education system since the 1970s, with the growth of private schooling sector. In 2000, Australia (76%) and Japan (75%) ranked only behind the United States (68%) in terms of the large public share of educational expenditure (Gittins & Tiffen, 2004: 120). Government subsidising of private schooling has had the unintended effect of improving the quality of private schools, rather than their affordability, resulting in increased numbers of students from low-socioeconomic and migrant backgrounds in government schools (Ryan & Watson, 2005).

Most of the children in this study were local residents, many of whom lived in government housing. This housing typically consists of small three-bedroom cottages, each on their own suburban block, and often located along the busy main roads. It is typically allocated to refugees, migrants and the unemployed.

This form of housing is in line with Australia's unusual propensity to suburbanisation, in contrast with the high-density urban residential environments seen in major cities elsewhere. Owning property on free-hold land became accessible to many during the suburban boom of the 1870s and 1880s, when high wages and steady employment provided opportunities for the working class – now known in the rhetoric as 'working or ordinary Australians' (Rolfe, 1998).

Home ownership, complete with a backyard and Hills Hoist (rotating umbrella-shaped washing line) in sprawling suburbia, is the 'Australian dream' (Burnley et al., 1997). Yet at the same time, life in the suburbs is geographically and socially stratified.

With the rising demand for land close to the central business districts, and gradual 'suburban' renewal, those living in the outer suburbs are typically less affluent than inner and middle suburban dwellers. The school in this study was situated in a low-socioeconomic suburb. Of the occupied residential dwellings being rented, 29.8% were rented from a State housing authority, contrasting the figure of 14.9% Australia wide (Australian Bureau of Statistics, 2006).

Public Schooling and Diversity

For example, Zak would meet me at the school gate with his wide grin revealing his decayed teeth from years of neglect. He knew me from the community centre I used to run voluntarily after school in a local hall. During the time I ran the centre, his father died in a drunken brawl. Zak and his older sister Michelle lived on the main road in a housing commission area near the school. They would often wander the streets dirty and hungry, or on payday, eating lollies and potato crisps. Zak and Michelle were frequently unable to go home after the community program because their drunken mother would swear and shout abusively at them (and me) when they neared the house.

The primary school they attended had been operating for over a century, reflected in the architecture of the buildings. The typical 'Queenslander' style wooden structures of the early 1900s were built on stilts, containing a row of classrooms on the top floor with doors on the length of the building and windows along the other. Unlike most government buildings in Queensland, public school classrooms are rarely air-conditioned, making them unbearably hot in summer, noisy during storms and cold during the brief winter.

On the front of the buildings, the classrooms are adjoined by a long veranda or covered external walkway to block the rain but not the breeze, which runs the full length of each building leading to a staircase at either side. The primitive ground floor is an 'undercover' area used for eating morning tea and lunch, and playing handball, hopscotch or skipping, without complete walls, with a cement floor in which wooden benches are bolted to the floor and water troughs are set on the periphery called 'bubblers' to hydrate students.

Like many Queensland schools, the 'tuck shop' was situated underneath one end of these buildings with a typical tin roller-door above the front counter to serve students. The tuck shop is where simple fast food such as sandwiches, meat pies and drinks are prepared, purchased and sold by parent volunteers, and made available for student purchase for those who can afford to do so.

The school, like most public schools in the country, did not provide free lunches to even the poorest students. Many of the students in the school came to school without having eaten a healthy breakfast. For example, an Indigenous Australian student was observed stealing a portion of unwrapped, unrefrigerated cheese – supplied by peers for filming a claymation movie – and pocketing it in his tracksuit. The misshapen, sticky lump constituted his lunch.

The school community was composed of diverse cultures and schooling experiences. Twenty-five ethnic groups were represented in the school's clientele, from 24 suburbs. Some 8% of the school's students were Indigenous Australians, a historically disadvantaged group, socially and economically, which is significantly higher than the 2.2% of Indigenous persons represented in the Australian population (Australian Bureau of Statistics, 2003).

During the year of the pilot study, the school population of students for whom English was a second language (ESL) was 7%. Immigration is a major contributor to the Australian population growth, making up 22% of the total population (4.1 million residents) in the 2001 census (Australian Bureau of Statistics, 2003). One of the explicit visions of the school, according to a statement in the unpublished School Community Profile, was to 'achieve the best possible educational outcomes for all our students ... through equity of educational opportunity'.

An impetus for this monograph is that the early 21st century is characterised by significant cultural and linguistic diversity in schools and society, creating the need for inclusive pedagogies. English has different national forms, dialects and registers, including subcultural groups with every conceivable interest, style and sense of affiliation. Consequently, literacy teaching that focuses on a single national 'standard' and simplistically 'correct usage' is redundant, while the negotiation of difference is essential. Assimilating immigrants and indigenous peoples to the standardised 'proper' language of the coloniser – a goal that was promulgated in former times – now seems glaringly inadequate (Cope & Kalantzis, 1999).

The clientele of Australian schools is drawn from an increasingly diverse mélange of ethnic, community and social class cultures, with a wide range of texts, interests and group identities. English is becoming a world language, yet it is breaking into multiple and increasingly differentiated 'Englishes', marked by accent, dialect or subcultural differences tied to membership in communities such as professional, recreational, sporting or peer groups (Cope & Kalantzis, 2000b). Those who are most successful in life are those who are competent to negotiate real differences, code switching between multiple semiotic systems and hybrid, crosscultural discourses for varied communication purposes (New London Group, 2000).

Not only this, but the emerging communications technologies generate new forms of digital text that increasingly multimodal – combining linguistic, visual, auditory, gestural or spatial modes. Yet in this school, only 77% of the students had access to a computer at home, according to a school-based survey. This figure only represents the physical presence of computers in homes, and does not illuminate the differences in the quality and kinds of access afforded to various students in their homes. The students reported to me that their home computers often needed repair or replacement, and parents alone accessed others. Among the students who owned computers, most did not have home internet access. Beyond their homes, multimedia technologies, screen-based interfaces and electronic networks proliferate (Mills, 2008a; New London Group, 2000).

Multiliteracies Teacher

A colleague put me in contact with a group of teachers who had received professional development in multiliteracies through a scholarship project coordinated by original members of the New London Group – Kalantzis and Cope (2005: 179). Three teachers and 120 students across several school districts voluntarily consented to be involved in an initial pilot study that involved ethnographic observation of media-based lessons applying new pedagogies in routine school settings. After working with these teachers, I decided to focus the research on one school site, having amassed more video data than could be usefully analysed within a reasonable time by one researcher.

I collected the richest forms of data about multiliteracies from Jennifer, who demonstrated exemplary knowledge and expertise in teaching innovative literacy practices with new digital media. She had taught students, from early childhood to upper primary, how to design e-books, hyperlinked web pages, digital animations and movies. Jennifer had gained many years of international experience teaching literacy in culturally and linguistically diverse teaching contexts, including remote regions of outback Australia to inner city schools in the United Kingdom. She believed that teaching multiliteracies was an issue of priority in the new communications environment, and often talked about the daily challenges of negotiating cultural and linguistic diversity among the students and parents. She was a catalyst for demonstrating to other teaching staff how to engage students in creative and critical uses of the new media.

Jennifer talked about the challenges of negotiating cultural and linguistic diversity among the students and their parents. For example, she used a Sudanese translator to communicate with the parents of the refugee students. She was clearly a teacher with exceptional skills in teaching new digital media to students of all ages, and I was impressed by her creative teaching ideas. Her enthusiasm and energy for innovation and curriculum change were inspirational.

Multiliteracies Class

I initially spent 160 hours of continuous journal writing, and audio and video recording, building my knowledge of how the teaching of multiliteracies was integrated across the curriculum and routine practices of schooling in a normative context. This time was invaluable for building rapport with Jennifer, who became comfortable with my continual presence in the room, and the data collection procedures. The subsequent year to the pilot study, I began the research proper with her upper primary class, which was streamed by the school according to the results of a standardised literacy test (Queensland Studies Authority, 2007b). The class consisted of the 23 lowest-ability students in the total year group – eight girls and 15 boys.

The class comprised students from mixed socioeconomic and ethnic backgrounds, including Anglo-Australian, Tongan, Thai, Aboriginal, Maori, Sudanese and Torres Strait Islander students. No longer is the Australian classroom comprised mostly of Anglo-Saxon, monolingual users of English who are being prepared for a predominantly monocultural workplace. Rather, in schools, society and globally, effective communication requires negotiating multiple Englishes and communication patterns that cross subcultural and national boundaries (Lo Bianco, 2000).

I conducted one-on-one interviews with a culturally diverse group of students to gain comparative data about their home and school literacies, including uses of new digital media. An interesting student whom I observed and interviewed was Daria, a tall girl in early adolescence, who had immigrated to Australia as a Sudanese refugee when she was four years old – the start of her formal schooling. In Sudan, she spoke two languages in the home, Sudanese Arabic and a local vernacular, Otto-tana. Daria's discourses used in the home included a rich variety of multilingual and multimodal textual practice, using three languages interchangeably – English, Arabic and Otto-tana. She had good spoken English skills, which she always supplemented with rich use of gestures. Daria assimilated well with her peers, demonstrating leadership skills throughout the collaborative claymation work. Daria read 'chapter books' and magazines at home every day for at least 10 minutes, and always completed her homework. She loved drawing and her family owned a computer with facilities for English–Arabic translation. When I asked what she would like to be as an adult, she said, 'modelling'. Daria was one of many Sudanese refugees in the school whom the teacher described as 'fresh off the boat'. The families of these students were non-English speaking, increasing the complexity of providing access.

Ted was Indigenous Australian, and lived with his single mother and extended family, and with his uncle for part of each week. Ted was an intriguing student whose precocious and amiable nature constantly drew my attention as an ethnographic observer. He was the first student to welcome me, and he talked very openly about his home life. His antics to attract the teacher's attention during direct instruction caused continual disruption to the flow of lessons, though these intrusions were seemingly well intended. Ted reported that he never read books at home, and he could not name a single book title. His family did not own a computer, and he indicated that he could not do homework when he visited his uncle, because they often arrived home at midnight.

Schools have a historical role in the reproduction of social inequity, both allowing and preventing access to literacies and its associated power to alternatively gain or miss out on social mobility, wealth and professional status (Bourdieu, 1977). Literacies have been distributed unequally on the basis of gender, class, ethnicity, geographical location (e.g. urban versus rural), disability and combinations of these social characteristics (Kress, 1993). For example, studies have consistently identified achievement gaps between students from Anglo-Saxon, middle-class backgrounds and minorities such as African Americans (Heath, 1983), urban poor (Farkas, 1996), Indigenous Australians (Bourke *et al.*, 2000), Maori (Bishop, 2003; Cazden, 1992), students from remote geographical areas (Khattri *et al.*, 1997), and those from low-socioeconomic backgrounds (McLaren, 1994). Clearly, access to literacies – new or old – is tied up in the politics and power relations of everyday life in literate cultures (Luke & Freebody,

1997). Students like Daria and Ted are those who have historically been least-served by a Western educational system.

Similarly, Meliame was a multilingual, Tongan student who had immigrated to Australia a year and a half prior to the research. Her parents had returned to Tonga for business, while she remained in Australia with her brother, under the care of her aunt and uncle. At school, Meliame exhibited a compliant nature in class, worked productively on assigned tasks, but rarely contributed to whole class discussions. She diligently completed her homework each afternoon and then read novels. Television viewing was only permissible when her work was done. Her aunt and uncle did not own a computer, but her father had taught Meliame how to send emails before he left for Tonga.

Joshua was a monolingual, Anglo-Australian student from a low-socioeconomic background who had learning and behavioural problems. Joshua was seated at the front of the room at an isolated desk, rather than at desk clusters like most of the other students. This is because his attention-seeking behaviour, such as exaggerated movements and noise, were incessant. Joshua reported that reading at home occurred about once a month, and the only writing he engaged in at home was recording phone messages and drawing. His family owned a computer, and his older sister had taught him how to create some graphics. His dream was to work at McDonalds when he grew up, because you earn 'a lot of money'.

It was apparent that the students did not exclusively invent their attitudes and uses of multiliteracies at school. Instead, they drew upon different cultural resources or funds of experiences built into their lives outside of school, built up historically within their communities. The established norms and rules for multiliteracies in students' homes and the attendant cultural dimensions of students' lives were not the same, and thus, they came to school with entirely unequal possibilities for school performance.

The New London Group envisaged that a pedagogy of multiliteracies can potentially provide '... access without people having to erase or leave behind different subjectivities' (New London Group, 2000: 18). Pedagogy was visioned as '... a teaching and learning relationship that creates the potential for building learning conditions leading to full and equitable social participation' (New London Group, 1996: 60).

This is achieved by moving from a standard, national or universal culture to foster productive diversity that acknowledges the multilayered lifeworlds of students. They argued that a pluralistic worldview, not a tokenistic one, is the only way that the educational system can '... possibly be genuinely fair in its distribution of opportunity, as between one group and another' (Kalantzis & Cope, 2000b: 125). They highlighted dramatic global changes to public, community and economic life, envisaging a multiliteracies pedagogy as a way to reduce the vast disparities in life chances for learners.

In the light of these tensions, I sought to investigate the possibility that the multiliteracies pedagogy might increase equity. Existing classroom-based research had not empirically examined the New London Group's pedagogy in terms of its provision for equitable access. Empirical research was needed to take into account the relations between pedagogy, modes, media, spaces, discourses and power used in the classroom, and the structures of power and agency in society, which operate to prevent or permit access to multiliteracies.

For example, the Australian government has initiated the National Assessment Plan for Literacy and Numeracy (Queensland Studies Authority, 2007a). Such basic skills testing regimes create tensions for teachers who are caught between emphasising a narrow band of print-based literacy skills that 'count' in comparative measures, over authentic, creative, productive and critical media practices that are required for success in the new communications environment.

This research explores the potentials of new pedagogies to transform the inequitable distribution of literacies, investigating whether inequities are simply reproduced, legitimised or otherwise contested by innovative pedagogies and new technologies in an institutional context where teaching print-based literacy practices are high on the agenda of the state government.

There is a need for a broader range of literacies and pedagogies to transform the existing selective transmission of knowledge, and the distribution of social opportunities to the dominant culture (Cook-Gumperz, 1986: 7). These new directions in literacy teaching require original research to interrogate whether or not inequities are reproduced, contested and legitimated within the unchartered waters of new pedagogies. Such research must ask questions about whose values, beliefs and interests are served by contemporary literacy pedagogies (Apple, 1997; Giroux, 1990; Street, 1993). This opens up a rich field of inquiry that interests educators, learning theorists, sociologists, experts of new digital media and communication, parents and policy makers.

The students in the school were not unaffected by the proliferation of new media and popular texts used in society. While the school prohibited the use of mobile phones, lessons would often be interrupted by the ringtones of devices that had been smuggled into the classroom. Teachers were required to confiscate the phones and appropriately discipline students. I observed lower primary girls cutting images of Britney Spears from the front cover of popular magazines that they had brought from home. Seven-year-old boys sung the lyrics of the American rapper, Curtis James Jackson, known by his stage name '50 Cent'. Boys made intertextual references to popular movies, such as *Shrek* and *Lord of the Rings*, and played Pokémon video games on their Nintendos.

The students were part of a broader historical shift from textual culture of print, to one in which the visual mode is salient, assisted by novel technologies that have become a resource for students' self-production. For example, the students' identities were carefully projected through the personalised ringtone of their mobile phones and the pop downloads on their MP3 players.

One of the aims of multiliteracies is to engage with the varied subjectivities of students, recruiting these as resources for learning, to unlock the gate of possibility for improved access (New London Group, 2000). It matters considerably if popular and digitally mediated literacies are acknowledged in literacy pedagogy and research.

Multiliteracies matters to students today, who need access to a broadened range of textual practices and media platforms than students of the past. Multiliteracies matters to teachers, who see the vast disparities among learners, yet know that how they teach makes a significant difference in the lives of their students. Multiliteracies matters to everyone in increasingly multicultural, globalised and digitally dependent societies.

Self-Reflexivity

Reasonable judgement should be used when making generalisations from this investigation to other settings. This is because similarities and differences between research contexts should be taken into account (For the generalisability of results in qualitative research, see Berg, 2004; LeCompte *et al.*, 1992). For example, the results were mediated by the teacher's personal conceptualisation and enactment of the multiliteracies pedagogy, the individual actions of students in her culturally and linguistically diverse class, and the system relations between classroom structures and institutional structures in the social milieu.

There is also a requirement of critical research to strive to maintain equal power relations between the researcher and the research participants. A genuinely interdependent relationship was sought between the researcher and the teacher, from the first meeting to the recursive dialogue about the findings. While the ideal of democratic research was upheld throughout the conduct of this research, I cannot claim that the truly equal generation of knowledge was fully attained. There can be no true parity of power between the researcher and the participants (Heron & Reason, 2001). I can only strive for self-reflexivity, examining my own contribution to dominance in spite of my intentions to liberate others (Lather, 1991; Mills, 2008b).

Given that no research can claim to maintain precisely equal power relations between researcher and participants, this report articulates how these differential relations served to benefit the participants. During the research, I showed Jennifer every lesson transcript (member checking), to allow her to challenge any misinterpretations, omissions, of the data by the researcher. Months after leaving the field, I carefully discussed a final summary of the research conclusions with the teacher over a meal to fortify the respondent validation of the research (see Berg, 2004; Maxwell, 2005).

This was enlightening for me. Although Jennifer had read all the lesson transcripts and agreed with the accuracy of record, she was able to provide an 'emic' or 'insider' interpretation of the events. This included events that occurred after the snapshot of data I had been privileged to encounter. Jennifer reflected that her pedagogies had been transformed by her involvement in this research and her concurrent involvement in the 'Learning by Design' project initiated by Kalantzis and Cope (2005).

In this way, unequal power relations were minimised. Moral respect for person is honoured when power is shared in the formation of knowledge about others. Any unavoidable differences between the roles of the researcher and the researched enabled us to consider 'life beyond the horizons of current experience' (Lather, 1990: 332).

Research Validity

An inevitable question that arises in judging the validity of a research report concerns the basis upon which events were included or excluded. I provide here a brief acknowledgement of how the data reported in this book were selected from the total corpus. Interested readers can consult a more detailed discussion of methodological issues elsewhere (see Mills, 2006c). While no research account can purport to be completely objective or value-free, certain methodological requirements were met to strengthen the validity of this study.

The criterion used to determine when the data sets were completed (observational and dialogical) was when the patterns of data were repeatedly reaffirmed until no new or relevant data about access to multi-literacies emerged for each coding category. For example, numerous lessons were observed that involved Jennifer's enactment of overt instruction, situated practice, and transformed practice in her pedagogies, rather than critical framing.

Because theoretical saturation was reached in these categories, I arranged to observe additional lessons to build up a more detailed record of critical framing. In this way, I reached the point-of-diminished-return, so that repeated patterns in her enactment of critical framing could be identified. In this way, claims reported in this account are supported by multiple and recurring observations of similar events over the course of the longitudinal study.

I transcribed and applied coding procedures to the entire body of data – every videotaped lesson, every audio-recorded conversation and every journal entry. In other words, both transcription and coding were applied comprehensively to the primary record, rather than in a selective way. This enabled me to have a complete record of events that was detailed enough for readers to know as much about the events as if they were present.

I used open coding to identify the key themes and meaning reconstructions, using comment boxes alongside the digitalised, written primary record. These raw codes were then organised and reordered into tighter hierarchical schemes.

The level of inference of the codes could be positioned along a continuum from low to high, or from pure descriptions using non-technical terms, to theoretical, abstract terms and meanings. An example of low-level coding is the category 'filming movies', which names an event observed. The high-inference codes were more theoretical, such as 'situated practice', 'discourses', 'coercive power' or 'marginalisation'.

During data analysis, a critical colleague read samples of the coding and analysis to challenge any degree of bias, and to clarify the appropriateness of the inference levels of the technical vocabulary. I then responded to this criticism to strengthen the validity of the coding. When all data sets had been coded and combined, I identified the 30 most frequently reoccurring themes in relation to understanding students' differential access to multiliteracies.

This process of coding was both inductive and deductive. The codes did not emerge from the data uninfluenced by pre-existing theory. Neither were the codes predetermined by the theory, since many of the themes in the literature were found to have limited relevance to the interpretation and explanation of the data. Rather, the process of theory building involved an ongoing dialogue between data and theory. Certain themes from the literature appeared in what was observed, along with new and explicit patterns of events that could be explained using the themes.

The final analysis and reporting of findings in this book centres on the themes that had the most significant bearing on the students' access to multiliteracies. These key themes are reflected in the following chapter and subheadings of this book.

I include original transcripts in sufficient quantity to provide readers with the participants' own categories and vocabulary. By placing heuristic importance on members' own categories, the data in this book can speak for itself.

Note

1. All names in this monograph are pseudonyms to protect the anonymity of the research participants.

Chapter 2
Situated and Explicit Pedagogy

This chapter provides a window into the classroom during digital movie-making lessons, exploring Jennifer's enactment of the multiliteracies pedagogy – situated practice, overt instruction, critical framing and transformed practice (New London Group, 2000). I also refer to the Learning by Design framework by the members of the New London Group, Kalantzis and Cope (2005). I consider how the students demonstrated the four knowledge processes in Learning by Design – 'experiencing', 'conceptualising', 'analysing' and 'applying' – in the dynamic context of animated movie making (Kalantzis & Cope, 2005: 72).

The New London Group has moved beyond pedagogies of the past, combining and transforming them to reframe innovative and relevant literacy pedagogy for the changing times. These pedagogies include Dewey's Progressivism (associated with whole language), transmission or direct instruction (associated with basic skills), critical literacy, and finally, strands of cognitive science that emphasise strategies for transferring situational learning from one context to another (New London Group, 2000). Applied in isolation, none of these pedagogies can provide students with sufficient access to the literacies that are required for meaningful participation in society.

The multiliteracies pedagogy of the New London Group has been described at length by others, and is only summarised here. Situated practice involves building on the life-world experiences of students, situating meaning-making in real-world contexts. Overt instruction guides students to use an explicit metalanguage of design.

Critical framing encourages students to interpret the social context and purpose of designs of meaning. Transformed practice occurs when students transform existing meanings to design new meanings (Mills, 2006a; New London Group, 1996).

These components of the pedagogy do not constitute a linear hierarchy, but may occur simultaneously, randomly or be '... related in complex ways … each may occur simultaneously, while at different times one or the other will predominate, and all of them are repeatedly revisited at different levels' (New London Group, 2000: 32).

Jennifer's aim for the lessons reported in this chapter was to enable learners to collaboratively design a claymation movie – an animation process in which static clay figurines are manipulated and digitally filmed to produce a sequence of images of life-like movement. The process occurs by shooting a single frame, moving the object slightly, and then taking another photograph. When the film runs continuously, it appears that the objects move by themselves. Popular claymation productions include *Wallace and Gromit* and *Chicken Run*.

The technique involved planning a storyboard, sculpting plasticine characters, designing three-dimensional movie sets and filming using a digital camera. After filming, the students recorded the sound, and digitally edited the movies with a teacher's assistance. The students were required to effectively communicate an educational message to their 'buddies' in the preparatory year level (aged 4½–5).

The movies were also presented at a school event for the parent community, having real, cultural purposes, and demonstrating the transformation of resources to create original, hybrid texts. See Table 2.1 for a schedule of lessons. These were mostly implemented outside of the routine English period, when students were grouped by ability on the basis of standardised literacy test results for different literacy programs. Other print-based literacy lessons were observed during the routine English period, which are reported elsewhere (Mills, 2005b).

Open-ended aspects of designing included choosing the genre, theme, message, number and type of scenes (e.g. indoor/outdoor), characters, events, set and prop materials (e.g. fabric, paint, sand), spatial layout, shot composition and duration of the movie. Audio elements could involve background music, digitally recorded speech, sound effects or combinations of these elements to accompany the moving images.

Title pages, credits and subtitles could include unlimited spatial layout options, backgrounds, fonts, colours, graphics and digital effects. When the teacher evaluated the movies, she considered the extent and value of creativity, the aptness of the movie to the target audience, the use of film-making conventions, group collaboration and the evidence of transformation of existing ideas to a new movie.

At the outset, it was apparent that these upper elementary students had limited prior experiences of multimodal and digital textual designing upon which to link new knowledge.

Table 2.1 Claymation movie-making production

Claymation movie-making	Time
View claymation movies Teacher displays movies from other students and discusses the strengths and weaknesses.	1 h
Critiquing claymation movies Teacher guides students to analyse critically and functionally the claymation movie *Chicken Run*.	1 h
Storyboard Discuss plan for movie plot, scenes and characters. Allocate roles. Record ideas using picture frames and labels. List materials required. Create movie title.	2¼ h/group
Set design Plan and create three-dimensional dioramas with backdrop, stage and props using real objects and mixed media.	4 h
Character design Create three-dimensional characters by sculpting plasticine on wooden figures or by using mixed media.	2 h
Rehearsing Rehearse movements and determine photo schedule. Set up filming area, matching set proportions to camera angles.	1½ h
Filming Take 60–200 digital photos of the movie sets using a tripod while moving the characters and objects gradually. Control lighting and position of the tripod. Change expressions and gestures of characters. Take close-ups and long shots.	2–4 h/group
Sound Write and rehearse script to match visual elements and/or select digital music files to match visual elements. Record script (speech) digitally using computer and microphone.	2 h
Digital editing Use digital software to combine images and sound files, and to create special effects, subtitles, title pages, credits and backgrounds.	½ h/group
Presenting movies to community	3 h

Source: Mills (2006b)

Has anyone here done claymation before? No – so it's a new process for you. For most of your literacy lessons so far in your education, you've probably done a lot of work from the blackboard, or writing stories or doing a bit of research. Not many of you have used multimedia – when you're using different types of media. So we'll be using computers. We'll be using digital cameras. We may be using scanners or CD players, and using different types of technology to do our literacy. I love using multimedia!

The students were given the opportunity to engage in designing that was radically different in many respects to their previous work dominated by conventional writing tools, and antiquated pedagogies, such as copying text from a blackboard. In the teacher's own words: 'The interesting thing about these kids is they have no background in this, so they've just got no idea'.

Overt Instruction: Conceptualising

The teacher guided the students in a discussion about a segment of the commercially produced claymation movie *Chicken Run*, which they had viewed moments before:

Teacher:	Sitting up nicely, ready to listen … What events happened in the movie? Great to see your hand up!
Harry:	I saw the chickens trying to go under the fence.
Teacher:	The chickens tried to go under the fence. What else happened in this plot?
Sarah:	They tried four times to get away.
Teacher:	Four times unsuccessfully. How else did they escape?
Nick:	Underground.
Teacher:	Underground. They're digging a hole underground or digging under the fence. What's another way they tried to escape? There are two more ways.
Mark:	When they were in the trough.
Teacher:	The trough?
Joseph:	Yes.
Teacher:	They were hiding underneath the trough where the legs were just going and they were trying to get out – upside down. Jack?
Jack:	They dressed up as a clay person.
Teacher:	Who were they dressed up as?
Children:	Mrs Teedie.
Teacher:	Oh, excellent!

I include the above transcript to demonstrate a typical pedagogy observed in Jennifer's lessons – transmission. The teacher controlled the topic using a form of direct instruction – a three-part 'IRE discourse – teacher Initiation, student Response and teacher Evaluation' – to assist students to recount the series of complications in the plot of the movie (Mehan, 1979). This common pattern of classroom discourse in Western schooling requires interactions by invitation of the teacher, often used for the purpose of introducing new content. Regulatory discourse was used to make explicit requirements for student posture (e.g. 'sitting up, ready to listen'), and gestures (e.g. '... hand up'), which positioned learners as listeners.

It was observed that when Jennifer's class was divided into two ability groups, direct instruction characterised 90% of instruction time with the lowest literacy ability students. For example, the first claymation lesson for the low-ability group exclusively applied direct instruction. The first lesson was a 50-minute multimodal display of other students' claymation movies, presented on a large screen. The teacher verbally outlined the step-by-step process as the students watched and listened. A transcript taken from the 300 lines of the teacher's dialogue is shown here to illustrate the form of instruction.

So, script writing – I have to approve the script. It has to be sensible. Remember our 'buddies' are going to see them. We have that book launch, and all of our guests are going to see them as well. Now, you have to make your characters. You get plasticine, pipe cleaners, googly eyes, those little wooden people, you can use puppets, you can use paper and you can use whatever you like – egg cartons, whatever you like to make the characters.

You also have to design your sets and paint them or maybe glue stuff to them. Some children last year got sand out of the sand pit and glued the sand to the bottom to make it look like a path. It was fantastic! They got real leaves out of the garden, and attached it to big plasticine, um brown trunks to make trees. You can see them when I show you the movies – really fantastic ideas!

The production part of it means you're going to be filming it with a digital camera. Then you need to decide which person's going to be the photographer. OK? So you have to work out who's going to be what. When you film it, you're going to have a tripod and your little set. Can you see that the set is really quite small? The set is about the size of a piece of cardboard. See this book – that's about the size of your set and you'll have a piece of cardboard flat on the ground and a piece of cardboard sitting up. That's about as big as it gets. So you don't need to make a huge set.

When Jennifer worked with the ability group that was closer to average, she used a more interactive pedagogy. The students were given the opportunity to dialogue with the teacher, asking questions about how the movies were made. The teacher qualified this differentiation between the two groups, explaining that due to timetable constraints she had insufficient time to guide the low-ability students to discover the answers. Normally, she would be highly interactive with the students and 'draw the information from them'. A key difficulty was that both ability groups had the same timetable allocation to learn the same concepts, which the teacher highlighted as a significant system constraint.

Teacher-centred transmission differs from the New London Group's description of overt instruction because it merely refers to expert to novice transmission of content. In contrast, overt instruction provides explicit information at times when it can most usefully guide the learners' practice (Mills, 2006a; New London Group, 2000).

The contrasting use of pedagogies with different groups of students is significant. The symbolic practice of ability grouping in the school served as a constraining form of differentiation, distributing different literacies to students in a marginalising way. The low-ability group received transmissive forms of pedagogy, used to regulate their behaviour and deliver content quickly. Yet transmissive pedagogies do not encourage decision-making, problem-solving or higher-level reasoning and critical thinking. These are the kinds of thinking skills that are needed for students to gain social mobility through professional careers. Few of the students in the low-ability stream were from white middle-class backgrounds. The school practice of ability grouping for English unintentionally contributed to a non-reflexive causal loop that sustained the unequal distribution of certain literacies for certain students (Mills, 2009).

Following the 50-minute introductory lesson, students in both ability groups were required to collaboratively prepare a storyboard or series of frames depicting the main events of their intended movie. A group of students were reading a large worksheet with the headings: 'Title', 'Characters', 'Photographer' and 'Scene', and a set of blank frames to design a visual storyboard of the movie narrative. David, Rose, Joseph (Anglo-Australians) and Paweni (Thai) were students from the low-literacy ability group.

David:	Who wants, ah?
Joseph:	What, what?
David:	Who wants to be the 'photo' 'grapher'? [Mispronounced]
Rose:	What's the 'photo' 'grapher'?
Joseph:	Let Rose be one.
Rose:	I don't want to be – pick Paweni.
Paweni:	No, no!
Rose:	Ok, I will. I will be the photographer.
David:	What characters?
Joseph:	I'll be, ah …

[Later]

David:	Who's the character? Who's the character?
Rose:	Um?
Joseph:	What's the characters?
Rose:	Characters, like um, like, I don't know!
David:	Everybody – you need everybody to be the character!
Rose:	Can you just wait! I've gotta get my, like …
David:	Um, I don't know everybody. You need everybody to be a character.
Rose:	With the like, characters, you need like, the name, and then …
David:	No, what are we doing first? What are we doing?
Joseph:	Yeah, what are we doing first?

Here, the students were required to negotiate the central elements of their claymation movie and determine their roles in production. Evidently, they were unfamiliar with the written notation of the metalanguage for claymation design. A metalanguage includes named concepts for referring to meaning-making elements of a textual practice – terms such as 'photographer' and 'characters' (Mills, 2006a).

While this process of engagement in the task caused a degree of cognitive disequilibrium that can lead to learning (resolution), the task exceeded the students' capacity to succeed or accommodate the new (van Eck, 2006). At the conclusion of this interaction, the students were unable to locate a suitable starting place for meaning-making (Mills, 2006a).

A group of Anglo-Australian boys, who were also from the low-literacy-ability group, encountered similar difficulties.

Simon:	What we should do, what we should do is just write the script first and then go back and draw all the pictures, and [interrupted]
Ben:	Yeah, that's a good idea, but how we gonna, but what happens if the person is too big for the new script, and we don't know how to draw it?
Tim:	Well, maybe we could draw it little.
Teacher:	Come on boys, why has someone not got a pencil, and why are you not actually writing your script! Don't waste any more time! You already wasted one day when I wasn't here.
Ben:	We should um [pause] we should um [pause]
Simon:	We should start writing the script.
Ben:	Ok.
Simon	I'm gonna write first [softly] I'm gonna write first? [loudly]
Tim:	Are you?
Ben:	What? Ah hmmm. Anyone got a ruler? I need a ruler.
Simon:	I'll get a ruler.
Tim:	So what are we gonna do first? [No answer from Ben. Long silence as they wait for Simon to return]
Simon:	Ok. I got the ruler.
Tim:	What are we gonna do first?
Simon:	Write the script.

These boys were unable to conceptualise the pre-filmic elements of claymation movie making. The use of transmission in the first claymation lesson was not all that was needed for Simon, Tim and Ben to begin work performed with available meanings in the semiotic process (Mills, 2006a). The tendency for teachers to draw upon transmissive pedagogy for low-ability learners, with its one-way, expert-to-novice dispensing of knowledge, has been observed in other studies (Burnett, 1995; Oakes, 1990).

While overt instruction has an important place in the multiliteracies pedagogy, it should be used at times when it can optimally guide students' practice. Effective 'overt instruction' refers to the sum total of active interventions by a teacher or expert that extend and utilise the learners' existing knowledge and skills (Kalantzis & Cope, 2000a).

During other prefilmic stages of design, such as set and character designing, some learners encountered difficulties realising the potentials and limitations of the new media and technologies. For example, Daria, who is Sudanese, began to draw an outline of the second scene as a distance shot of a park. She intended this to be visible behind a life-size sandwich on a tablecloth, which the group had drawn from a close-up, aerial perspective in their storyboard frames. Daria could not anticipate that the distant objects in the background, viewed from eye-level, would not be consistent with the representation of a sandwich taken from close-up, aerial persepctive (Mills, 2006a).

Teacher Aid: For scene number two, if you've got the focus on the sandwich, all you're going to see behind it is green grass. It will be really easy to do.

Daria: That's just gonna be grass? [Daria had proposed that the park would still be visible in the background of a close-up, aerial perspective shot of a sandwich.]

Teacher Aid: Yes, but to make it more interesting, you're going to put bugs and things in it, crawling around.

Julia: That will still look a bit boring, but.

Daria: Yeah, but that's weird because [long pause].

Teacher Aid: Look – like that [holds object in front of backdrop]. Whereas if you have a scene that's too far away, you'll have this giant sandwich next to these little details of the park!

Daria: Yeah, but then that's gonna be funny, because grass up there? [Points to the backdrop scene] Isn't there supposed to be grass underneath the mat?

Teacher Aid: Yes. But when you look at something close-up, from aerial perspective, the only scene behind it will be green grass.

Daria: It will be up like that? The camera will take the photo up like that? [At a 45° angle to the scene]

Teacher Aid: That's right. So you don't even need to draw a backdrop because that's all you can see [in the viewfinder].

Daria: So um, I don't get it. I get this one – I really do get this one [The first scene at the beginning of the movie which is a long shot of the park].

The principles necessary for Daria to internalise the understanding of shot types and its relation to set design were too complex to be adequately described. Backdrop designing required prerequisite knowledge of visual and spatial design, and camera angles. This knowledge was situated and heavily contextualised in the practice of filmmaking, most readily acquired through direct experiences with a digital camera and through analysing shot types. Daria was unable to understand the concept of shot types and its implications for the spatial and visual design of the set. The technical landscape of movie making was unfamiliar to Daria, who needed to see examples of shot types and digital camera work first hand (Mills, 2006a).

The direct instruction provided in the first lesson had involved learners in viewing completed claymation movies, with little discussion of shot types, to understand the movie-making process. Without physical examples of claymation sets with situated practice using a digital camera, the distance between the prior experiences of students like Daria, and the technology-mediated aspects of designing, was vast. The students needed to be transported into a world of designing that was somewhat familiar, and not too perplexing (Mills, 2006a).

Situated Practice: Experiencing

Ted, Daria and Julia talked as they designed clothing and accessories for the plasticine characters in their movies. They had planned their storyboard, movie set and some of their props in previous lessons.

Ted: Daria is still doing the …
Julia and Ted: Shoes!
Julia: She's started a new sandal-type fashion. [Smiles]
Ted: We've been wastin' a whole million watchin' her doin' her shoes.

Here, one student in the group was remodelling realistic miniature sandals for the clay figure, while the others observed. Daria's design of the main character's footwear had consumed more than an hour of class time. The task of designing plasticine clothing to adhere securely to a preformed wooden figure was both different and similar to the students' previous experiences with two-dimensional designing.

There were new material elements to negotiate in three-dimensional designing, such as weight, form, texture, consistency, malleability and adhesion. The pedagogy at work here was situated practice, as the students 'experienced the known' and made links to 'the new' (Kalantzis & Cope, 2005). Ted's comment, using his indigenous dialect – 'We've been wastin' a whole million watchin' her doin' her shoes' – alludes to a potential weakness of situated practice when enacted without certain learning conditions.

Research in cognitive science has shown that human thought is not simply a combination of decontextualised facts. Instead, knowledge is principally situated in sociocultural settings and fundamentally contextualised in specific practices and domains (Lave & Wenger, 1991; Mills, 2006d). For example, students learn best about film making through situated experiences in movie production, guided by an expert, rather than, say, writing about movie making.

These ideas are not unique to the New London Group, but were originally expressed by a number of theorists. For example, Lave (1988) and Lave and Wenger (1991) use the concept of 'situated learning' to describe induction into productive and participative societal practices. Literacy theorists such as Street (1995), Heath (1999) and Gee (1992) describe literacy as varied social practices in specific cultural contexts – situated literacies. Well-known approaches to literacy learning, such as whole language and process writing, which follow the progressive tradition of Dewey, also emphasise situated, real-world reading and writing experiences (Dewey, 1966; Mills, 2006d).

During situated practice, one of the significant challenges was to enable the students to make links to the unknown world of clay animation – to experience the known and the new. Drawing from Kalantzis and Cope's (2005) Learning by Design model, 'experiencing the known' involves making connections to familiar life-world experiences, texts, media and interests of learners. An example is when teachers ask children to share their experiences before introducing a text about a related topic (Mills, 2006d).

'Experiencing the new' is participation in new, life-like or authentic learning experiences (Mills, 2006d). For example, prior to digitally recording the claymation scripts, the teacher engaged the students in rehearsing their script using the microphone to become familiar with the new skills and technology. In order for learners to make intuitive links with prior knowledge, there must be some elements of familiarity in the new experiences.

With the exception of the first lesson showing claymation movies, the 15-lesson series (18 hours) was predominantly comprised of situated practice involving pre- to post-filmic processes of claymation movie making. Each lesson typically began with a short introduction of direct instruction followed by 50 minutes of collaborative group work. An example of a typical lesson introduction is provided in the following transcript.

> Today, you have time to start working on your set. I do not want you to start working on your characters yet, so you are not actually making any of your characters. That means your group should have two pieces of cardboard, paints and other materials. You are simply making the background and base, using your storyboard ideas. I do not want to see anybody just sitting around wasting time. You have two weeks to have this claymation finished. Your sets, your props and your characters have to be completely finished by next week. All right?

The lesson introductions principally served to organise the students and materials, outlining expectations and timelines. The teacher anticipated that the students would recall her instructions from the first lesson, or visit the permanent display table at the back of the room where a static display about claymation designing could be perused for ideas. With the support of peers, it was expected that the students would acquire claymation movie-making skills naturally and functionally by experimenting with different design choices.

Several transcripts are shown here to highlight the degree of learning that occurred in each of the six groups in varied stages of movie designing. For example, Sarah and Elizabeth, who are Anglo-Australians, Emma, who is Maori, and Meliame, who is Tongan, were designing clothing for their claymation characters. This required three-dimensional configurations of meaning using visual and spatial modes. The girls formed the characters according to their personal image, including identity markers such as eye colour, hair colour and style and fashion accessories.

Sarah: I'm *trying* to make a shirt [cutting a shirt shape as a poncho from green fabric. Emphasises 'trying' as if she is unsure that she will achieve her purpose]

Emma: It's really hard because you can't really, because when you put something on there, it's either too small or too big.

Researcher: Who's the shirt for?

Sarah: That – that! [Points to the tiny, wooden figure]

[Later in the lesson]

Meliame: [Meliame is experimenting with different design solutions. She is attaching two-dimensional paper clothing panels to the wooden character whose torso is a three-dimensional rectangular prism. Meliame uses the plasticine to adhere to T-shirt-shaped paper panels (front and back – no sides), leaving large gaps where the side seams cannot be joined]

[Days later]

Researcher: What happened to the green jumper that you made?

[The claymation character was dressed the previous week].

Elizabeth: Mrs Fulton [Teacher of another class] said that the clothes didn't look real because they looked like rags – things that are just stuck on.

These girls encountered certain design constraints when tailoring fabric garments for three-dimensional, jointed, wooden figures. The girls transferred their ability to draw two-dimensional shapes to a significantly different context – three-dimensional designing. The students recognised the inadequacy of their designs and materials to represent their ideas, but were limited in their abilities to develop design solutions. Over the course of several lessons and lunch hours, they engaged in multiple, collaborative transformations of the characters using plasticine, paper, fabric, tape, sewing pins, yarn, adhesive gum, ribbons and other materials.

The girls needed contextual clues, scaffolds or temporary support structures to enable them to apply their skills in this situated task (Kalantzis & Cope, 2000a). Capable peers, media artists from the community or powerful artefacts such as books, technology and other media could have been enlisted for this purpose (Brown *et al.*, 1993). The girls were eventually shown how to join the materials together effectively, but considerable learning time had already been spent pursuing unproductive paths.

Brown and Campione (1994) emphasise joint construction or guided participation of learning within a zone. They refer to Vygotsky's (1978) 'zone of proximal development', which denotes the difference in the level of social and cognitive attainments between a child working alone and a child engaged collaboratively in a task with the guidance of an adult (Mills, 2006d; Vygotsky, 1962). A key observation in this multiliteracies classroom was not that the tasks were beyond the zone of possible attainment, but that the appropriate degree of scaffolding by a more capable expert or technology was not always present.

The group who achieved the least during situated practice was the group of Anglo-Australian boys from the low-ability literacy stream, who created a script for 'Breaking News'. The teacher was mindful of the boys' learning and behavioural difficulties, and had placed them together to afford the highest level of scaffolding.

Teacher: What is the reporter saying?
Ben: In Hawaii there is a volcano happening [said softly, as if to himself]
Simon: [Looking at the storyboard]
Teacher: What do you mean 'volcano happening'? What's a better word to use than 'happening'?
Ben: Ah, destroying?
Teacher: Volcano *erupting* today? [The teacher proceeded to spell this word when Ben could not progress beyond 'er'.]

Ben was limited by his prior knowledge and experiences of writing conventions. For example, he had insufficient knowledge of the language of a television news report. Prior to this interaction, the teacher had given the boys an impromptu geography lesson explaining where volcanos and other natural disasters occur. This is because Jennifer identified that they required better knowledge of their chosen subject matter – volcanos. Ben also lacked the requisite technical vocabulary (e.g. erupting) and knowledge of orthography (e.g. spelling 'erupting').

Simon:	What about ash? [Makes whistling sound decreasing in pitch like fireworks.]
Teacher:	Come on – Simon! On task for heaven's sakes! Your concentration span – volcano!
Simon:	[Slowly writes 'volcano'.]
Teacher:	Right – the next picture. You want the volcano shaking and an earthquake. Did you want people in this picture?
Boys:	[Laughter].
Teacher:	Come on, Simon, move it! Gosh boys, you get off-task quickly!
Ben:	Two hundred people were injured, and one person was killed. [Reading back script and then making squeaking, rubbing sounds on the desk using nearby objects.]
Teacher [to the researcher]:	They are just completely off-task! I cannot keep them on-task. It's just too much effort.

These boys required an exceptionally high level of continual scaffolding throughout all stages of movie production, which was not sustainable for the teacher. The grouping arrangement began to prove unhelpful because the teacher's attention was divided between the needs of the other students who were simultaneously engaged in the specialist discourse of movie making for the first time (Mills, 2006d).

A salient characteristic of Communities of Practice is the use of 'distributed expertise' to make learning shared and collaborative (Brown *et al.*, 1993; Brown & Campione, 1994). For instance, the teacher could induct or apprentice groups of students into a specialist element of media design, such as storyboards, set and character design, filming or editing. The teacher then regroups the students, distributing an expert to each collaborative group of movie makers to mentor their peers in one area of expertise (Mills, 2010c).

Novices could internalise the understandings of experts through scaffolded, cooperative activity with people and technologies that function as structuring guides, rather than relying exclusively on the teacher (Gee, 2000). When combined with reflection and conscious critique of the tacit goals and values, such as the need for all group members to contribute to multiple dimensions of the task, powerful learning can occur.

Proximal Practice

I use the term 'proximal practice' to describe a pedagogy in which situated learning is combined with timely instruction and guidance. When situated practice is tied to overt instruction, provided by peers, other experts, artefacts or technologies, there is scaffolding that leads to learning.

Proximal practice requires that instruction and situated practice be enacted concurrently in a seamless way, rather than as separate components. Access to multiliteracies requires the amalgamation of acquisition and learning, of situated practice and overt instruction, rather than teacher-centred transmission or situated practice in their isolated forms. Again, it should be emphasised that situated practice and overt instruction can be related in complex ways, rather than enacted in a rigid sequence (New London Group, 2000).

Vygotsky's (1962, 1978) notion of scaffolding, upon which the multiliteracies pedagogy draws, is important here. Vygotsky indicated that the most effective learning is demonstrated when practice and instruction occur concurrently, with a reduced level of scaffolding as independent learning is attained. In this study, certain forms of immersion in media design were required alongside instruction to enable the learners to acquire new movie-making skills.

Proximal practice is demonstrated in the following interaction. The teacher guided David, Joseph and Paweni to digitally record the script to complement the moving images of their movie. Paweni had limited conversational English skills, having lived in Australia for less than a year, and continuing to speak Thai at home (Mills, 2006d).

Teacher: I know English is your second language, so this is hard for you: 'Look out for cars'. Maybe you need to say: 'Look out for cars, son' [to emphasise the sound of 's' on the end of 'car' – a sound which Paweni was omitting]. Try it again.

Paweni: 'Look out for cars, son!'

David: 'Ok, Mum'.

Teacher: All right. That's all you're saying, and then I'm stopping the recording.

Joseph: 'Oh, no! I hit a child! I shouldn't have been talking on the phone'.

Paweni: 'Oh, my son!' [Very dramatic]

Teacher: Very good, Paweni! Right, Joseph, I'm going to let you listen to yourself even though you know it was just a practice run. [Replays recording]

Teacher: Ok, let's do it one more time. See if you can get a little bit better.

Before and after each short recording, the teacher provided the students with timely instruction to scaffold their audio text. Proximal practice was demonstrated, alternating between relevant direct instruction and learners' situated practice, during a 50-minute period.

Occasionally, the teacher asked critical questions to focus the students' attention on the effectiveness of the audio recording for the intended listeners: 'Do you think the audience will understand that?' Jennifer's questions stimulated critical evaluation of whether competence had been reached (Mills, 2006d).

Demonstrating the affordances of the digital technology, the teacher and students recorded the sound files multiple times until they reached a 'collaborative level of competence' (Kalantzis & Cope, 2005: 95). An outstanding quality of all movies produced by the students was the effective combination of audio elements – recorded dialogue and narration, music and sound effects – in an erudite manner (Mills, 2006d).

Through channelled collaboration between teacher and novices, the students created new audio elements that were more complex than what they could achieve on their own. Through the collaboration that occurred between teacher, expert novices and novices, knowledge was communicated and circulated rapidly and effectively through engagement in a community of practice (Mills, 2006d).

Proximal practice required the strategic scaffolding or the provision of temporary support structures through experts to equip the students with the technical knowledge for creating new digital media. In digital movie making, scaffolding was necessary to achieve two important functions in the community of learning.

First, the number of possible paths of inquiry needed to be limited to reduce the collaborative pursuit of futile and inefficient directions of designing. For example, when students explored the design possibilities for character design, they needed more frequent signposts to show how different manufactured materials could be fixed together to best represent the identity markers of the characters (Mills, 2006d).

Second, attention needed to be drawn to the important design elements of movie making that were too isolated from the students' previous experiences for them to make these connections independently. Focusing the students' attention could have taken several forms, such as verbal directions from an expert peer, examples of movie products or small group workshops with the teacher (Mills, 2006d).

For example, early in the design process, the learners needed to manipulate tangible movie sets and three-dimensional characters, rather than only viewing completed digital films. As such, productive situated practice would have been established using helpful exemplars (Brown, 2005). The immense challenge for teachers of multiliteracies is to create a community of practice where situated and scaffolded learning occurs like a lighthouse that guides vessels through unchartered waters, where students are prevented from 'wastin' a whole million' (Mills, 2006d).

Chapter 3
Critical and Creative Pedagogy

Teacher: … You don't have to agree with the author. That's the beauty of books …

Most children and youth today have ready access to a host of consumer-driven media, print and online texts from a much wider range of sources than previous generations. While situated practice and overt instruction are important, neither of these addresses the need for critical literacy skills. When used alone, these pedagogies can become socialising agents that encourage learners to be uncritical and unconscious of the cultural origins and worldview that underpins both texts and the social practices surrounding their production and use (Kalantzis & Cope, 2000a).

Children who are old enough to be entertained by videos and television programs need the conceptual tools to understand, select, challenge and evaluate the messages of texts, and to recognise who benefits from the media they consume. For example, even a child who demands yoghurt packaged with images of their favourite TV characters can realise that packaging does not make the yoghurt taste any better. Critical literacies can be used to explore alternative ways to read texts – to 'second guess' them, in ways that reposition students as active, critical agents, rather than as passive automatons (Luke & Freebody, 1999).

Critical literacy gives teachers tools to facilitate essential thinking processes, showing that literacy learning and texts are not neutral. Decisions about which texts are selected for children, and how media is used in homes, classrooms, commercial and recreational contexts are influenced by the beliefs and values of particular cultures and communities. Students need to discerningly analyse, evaluate and challenge assumptions about boys, girls, teenagers, adults, parents, groups and races that are either implicit or explicit in the texts and media they consume (Mills, 2005a).

Critical Framing

Drawing upon critical literacy, the New London Group use the term 'critical framing' to describe how readers and viewers make connections between the content of the texts they consume and the social contexts and purposes of those texts (New London Group, 2000). For example, when viewing a breakfast cereal advertisement, children can ask themselves questions about the target market of the product. They can begin to understand how certain words, images, music, gestures and animations are chosen very deliberately to influence children and the household shopper to select one competing cereal over another.

Kalantzis and Cope use the term 'analysing' as a way of describing what learners do during critical framing – the knowledge processes that occur (Kalantzis & Cope, 2005: 114). Analysing involves examining the discreet structure and function of represented meanings. The aim is for students to do two things – analyse functionally and analyse critically. Firstly, students analyse the overarching function of the everyday texts they read or view, making connections between the multimodal elements – 'analysing functionally' (Kalantzis & Cope, 2005: 114). For example, students might analyse and compare the differing roles, functions and purposes of diagrams and words in instructional texts, such as computer help menus, recipes and model-making books.

More importantly, they analyse the explicit and implicit agendas and interests behind a text – 'analysing critically' – whether it be a video game, billboard graphic or internet fansite (Kalantzis & Cope, 2005: 114). For example, students might analyse the gendered use of colour, font styles and images in toy packaging for boys and girls. In this section, I focus on the degree to which the teacher's enactment of critical framing enabled learners to analyse designs both critically and functionally, including analysing their own movies.

Analysing functionally

In several lessons, Jennifer used careful questioning sequences to prompt the students to functionally analyse the representations of power and other values embedded in commercially produced movies and books (Kalantzis & Cope, 2005). In the following transcript, the students had viewed several segments of the popular stop-motion animation *Chicken Run* by Aardman Animations, producers of the *Wallace and Gromit* films.

Teacher:	When the door opened and Mrs Tweedie was standing there, the light spilled out onto the steps. Why did they use the lighting in that way? What effect did it give her that she was in shadow and the bright light coming behind her when it panned up her leg?
Jack:	Strong.
Teacher:	Yeah, it made her look powerful!
Ted:	Scary.
Teacher:	She did look a bit scary. Ok, how did the creators show that Mrs Tweedie was in power? How did they show that she was the boss, Nick?
Nick:	The expression.
Teacher:	The expression on her face. Did you hear the dog yelp? The door opened and the dog went? [Child barks] Yeah, and did a little yelp – which means that he was definitely scared. What did you think?
Daria:	She had her hand on her hip.
Teacher:	Her hands were on her hips. Her body language showed that she was really very important.
Matthew:	She yelled, 'What is this chicken doing here?'
Teacher:	So, what she said was important.
Julia:	You could see her face and her head.
Teacher:	Think of the angle. Where was she? Where are they? [The chickens] What did the creators do to make her look more powerful, Ted?
Ted:	Looking up [camera angle].
Teacher:	They were looking up at her, and she was looking?
Students:	Down.
Teacher:	Down. This made them look as if they were quite small.

The teacher used a series of strategic questions and responses to guide learners to analyse functionally how power was represented through lighting ('Why did they use the lighting in that way?'), facial expression ('The expression on her face') and bodily movements or gestures ('Her body language showed that she was really important').

They also analysed functionally the sound ('Did you hear the dog yelp?'), speech ('So what she said was important'), and spatial elements, such as camera angles, spatial relations between characters and how the viewer is positioned ('Think of the angle. Where is she? Where are they?'). These questions encouraged students to analyse how the movie and its multimodal elements function to achieve the producers' purposes (Kalantzis & Cope, 2005).

This critique of the movie involved critical engagement and multiple readings that extended beyond linguistic design (written and spoken words). The students also attended to the spatial, visual, audio and gestural elements that work harmoniously to create meanings of significance. Through this functional analysis of multimodal design elements and their dynamic connections, the deeper meanings of the movie were illuminated.

During the same lesson, the teacher guided the students to retell the sequence of events in the movie plot. Through discussion, she assisted the students to analyse functionally the textual features of narratives. The teacher concluded the lesson with the following recommendations for the students' own narrative writing:

Teacher: This is my point. The stories that you are writing, some of them are very good, but you are not telling us enough exciting things. In your narratives, we want to see more details. In the first five minutes of the movie, look how many major plots and subplots happened. The movie hasn't even started and all of these things happened in the opening scene. You should start to think about making your plot more interesting, creating tension. Do you know what tension means? What is tension in a story?

Child: Build up.

Teacher: It's the build up. It's the climax of the story. It's the nail biting part of the story. It could be the music. It could be words like 'suddenly' to create a little bit of tension in your story.

The teacher had observed the need for the students to develop sophisticated plots in their compositions and storyboards. There was a need for multiple complications that build towards a climax and resolution of their tales. The teacher provided examples of audio design elements that could function to create a climax of a movie – 'It could be the music'. She also demonstrated how linguistic meanings could be used to create tension in written narratives – 'It could be words like "suddenly"'. Through this dialogue, the students were prompted to analyse functionally the multimodal elements of a mature narrative text and relate this new knowledge to their own designs.

Analysing critically

A second kind of analysis is necessary in critical framing – analysing critically. Analysing critically is a process of cross-examining human intentions and vested interests in a design. Questions can be asked about whose point of view is represented, and what the social and economic consequences could be (Kalantzis & Cope, 2005).

Jennifer was aware of these goals for critical framing. She conducted a lesson aimed to help students to identify and articulate the message and social values inscribed in a well-known picture book, *Lester and Clyde* (Reece, 1976). To prepare them for this discussion, the students had read the book in small groups with the support teacher earlier that day. Also prior to the excerpt shown below, the teacher had read how two frogs – Lester and Clyde – had moved from their initial pond, which had become polluted with refuse, to reside in a pristine freshwater habitat.

Teacher:	This is the other thing that I want you to think about. It says, 'Then Lester asks Clyde, "Why is it, if frogs really care, that men pollute ponds, and foul up clean air? They say we're no beauties, the poor mixed up lot, what do they know of beauty, what cheek have they got?" And Clyde shook his head saying of all he had heard, "What a crime!" he croaked loudly, "It's simply absurd, but although it's so wrong, at least we're safe here until …"'" [Turns page to show the picture of a bulldozer]
Students and Teacher:	'Man comes along!'
Teacher:	What can you see from the picture? What is the author trying to tell you? Simon?
Simon:	[Incoherent answer with long pauses]
Teacher:	What's going to happen to their pond? Sit up John Jackson. Don't chat. [Responds to Simon] Got it all confused up in your head? Daria?
Daria:	Um, the humans have got a machine; so they're going to wreck it.
Teacher:	The people are going to wreck it? Yes. Do you think that's a really good way for the author to end the story?
Students:	No.
Teacher:	To have them happy and back together again but, 'Dant-de, dant-de [Hums scary music from movie 'Jaws'].
Students:	Yes [Imitate the teacher's tune]

The teacher paused after reading the word 'until', which signalled to the students to predict the next event in the plot. The students followed her cue, reading in unison the important phrase, 'Man comes along'. Jennifer then focused their attention on the visual elements of the text to identify the author's environmental message: 'What can you see from the picture? What is the author trying to tell you?'

When the students demonstrated an inability to identify the author's message (not to pollute the environment), she focused instead on establishing requisite understanding of events in the plot. Her third question, 'What's going to happen to their pond?' was aimed to help the students infer that the bulldozer would destroy the pond. Daria's response showed her understanding of human intent to destroy the pond, which was signified by the machine.

Having established the prerequisite understanding of the bulldozer's significance to the storyline, Jennifer tried to refocus their attention on analysing the author's intended message of the text. To maintain the students' engagement in the lesson, she shifted from a teacher-centred, whole-class model of instruction to stimulate multiple discussions among pairs of students.

Teacher:	I'd like you to have a little whisper to someone around you. Hang on – I want you to wait for the question. The question is, just wait! The question is: 'Why did the author want that [points to the approaching bulldozer] to end the story. What was the author trying to tell you – the audience?' Have a little whisper to someone around you – see if you can find the answer.
Children:	[Students turn to the nearest student for 10 seconds of talking].
Teacher:	Why was the author wanting to have 'dant-de, dant-de' [music again] – tractor coming along? What was his point? I don't hear much whispering going on – I'm seeing a lot of people sitting there. [Ted and others have hand up to respond, and some are looking at the teacher]
Ted:	We've done it.
Harry:	All rubbish.
Teacher:	Excuse me – I haven't asked you yet. All right, Joshua and Harry – What did you come up with?
Joshua:	They need somewhere else to dump the rubbish.
Teacher:	They – the humans – want somewhere else to dump the rubbish; so they're moving onto the fresh pond? OK. What do you think Ted?
Ted:	Ah, they're gunna wreck the pond, and just like, put all oil and [interrupted]

Teacher:	My question was, 'Why did the author want you to think that?'
Support Teacher:	I had that problem too. I was asking the question, but the answer I got wasn't always the answer to the question.
Teacher:	They're not thinking about the author. We know that this is coming along to wreck the pond – we know that! Why did the author put it there? What's he trying to convince you of? What opinion is he trying to make you have?

In this discussion, the teacher repeatedly reformulates her question to guide the students to identify the author's intentions:

(1) 'What was the author trying to tell you – the audience?'
(2) 'Why did the author want you to think that?'
(3) 'Why did the author put it there?'
(4) 'What's he trying to convince you of?'
(5) 'What opinion is he trying to make you have?'

The students' responses indicate that they were unable to interpret the social and cultural context of the story. They could not stand back from meanings and view them critically in relation to the author's purpose and the intended cultural message for the readers – children, parents and teachers.

Joshua's response, 'They need somewhere else to dump the rubbish', and Ted's response, 'Ah, they're gunna wreck the pond, and just like, put all oil and ...' demonstrate that the students were unable, at this point in the lesson, to understand that there was an underlying social message in the storyline. They were still trying to grasp the immediate significance of the bulldozer in the plot of the narrative.

Teacher:	Rose?
Rose:	Um, because like, it's kind of like, the other pond has all rubbish and everything. And that's sort of like, he said that then it's gunna happen to their [new] pond.
Teacher:	So the author is trying to tell you that the same thing is going to happen to their [new] pond, unless what? [Deepens voice, as if becoming frustrated]
Rose:	Um, he stops throwing rubbish
Teacher:	Who stops throwing rubbish?

Rose and other voices: Humans.
Teacher: Human beings! So what is the author trying to tell you?

These upper elementary students experienced considerable difficulty analysing critically. The teacher drew upon Rose's response to explain that the author has an intended message for humans about care for the natural environment. Rose's response, 'He stops throwing rubbish', indicates a misunderstanding of the storyline, because she assumed that the frog was responsible for the garbage.

Rather than simply telling the students the environmental message of the text, the teacher wanted to draw this from the students. This was not easy conceptual work, since analysing the author's intentions was beyond what the children knew and could do independently.

Teacher: I need you to think. Why is the author telling you about the environment? He's telling us about polluting the pond. So why did he write this book? What did he want children to think? Simon?
Simon: Trash, (pause) put ... pollution
Teacher: Trash put pollution? What do you mean?
Simon: [Silence]
Teacher: OK. Start it again.
Simon: [No response]
Teacher: Harry?
Harry: Don't pollute the earth.
Teacher: That's right! This author wrote a lovely book about two fat frogs who had a fight, because he wants you to get the point about not polluting the earth ...

Forty minutes into the lesson, Harry was able to identify the social meaning underlying the narrative. He could understand that the author had another purpose beyond the general goal to entertain his readers. Having successfully prompted the students to identify the author's message of environmental stewardship, the teacher moved to another important dimension of analysing critically – to identify viewpoints or social practices in relation to their own values (Kalantzis & Cope, 2005).

Teacher: That's right. This author wrote a lovely book about two fat frogs that had a fight, because he wants you to get the point about not polluting the earth. Do you agree with him?
Children: Yes.

Teacher: You do agree? You don't have to. You don't have to agree with the author. That's the beauty of books. Do you agree that we should stop polluting?

The teacher helped the students to consider that they do not have to believe or agree with everything they read in a text. While the teacher did not outline possible alternative perspectives, she invited the students to go beyond an uncritical acceptance of the environmental message. The provocation hinted at the potential to express a diversity of opinions, rather than uncritically accept the author's perspective as a value-neutral truth. When alternative reading positions and practices for questioning and critiquing texts and their social assumptions are dormant, teachers assume a reproductive model of meaning.

The teacher explained to me after that the lesson that she had planned to address the following series of critical framing questions, translating them into a more accessible vocabulary for her students:

(1) What is the purpose of the text?
(2) Who has produced the text?
(3) For whom was the text created?
(4) Do the visual features of the text relate to the written text?
(5) What does the author want us to believe?
(6) What views are being put forward?
(7) Do the visual features of the text depict stereotyping of characters?
(8) Who is disadvantaged from the way the text is presented?
(9) Who has been left out of the text? Why?
(10) What possible meanings can be constructed from this text?
(11) What is the text trying to do to me?
(12) Which views are silent or absent?

Jennifer commented that the students had taken considerable time to understand the author's underlying agenda in the book. This meant that the critical framing questions were unable to be addressed in this lesson frame. However, the text was shown to represent a particular point of view, which was open to critique. Without critical pedagogy of this kind, comprehension becomes cultural assimilation, bringing readers' epistemologies into alignment with a corpus of historically valued knowledge.

As the lesson continued, the teacher prompted the students to consider the intended audience of the book, locating the message of the text in relation to their own values (Kalantzis & Cope, 2005).

Teacher: Do you think this is a book worth reading to the other children?

Children:	Yes.
Teacher:	Who else should read this book? Jack?
Jack:	Adults.
Teacher:	Adults should read this book?
Rose:	Everyone should. And like that pond – that's how our earth will end up.

The teacher guided the learners to make a personal appraisal of the book's worth. Without pre-empting by the teacher, the students concluded that the environmental message of the text – not to pollute the earth – was a message also applicable to adults, and indeed, everyone. Rose demonstrates a deeper understanding of the text than earlier in the lesson, insightfully interpreting the frog's pond as an analogy for the earth.

Another lesson serves to demonstrate how Jennifer guided the students to analyse critically – to interrogate the underlying intentions and interests of movie authors and producers. Prior to interactions below, the teacher had shown the students segments of the popular animated movie *Chicken Run*. She had replayed certain scenes and addressed key questions, which were reviewed in the following discussion.

Teacher:	What is the message that the movie creators are trying to get across to you? What does he really want you to think about during this movie, Ted?
Ted:	Not to stop trying.
Teacher:	You're not to stop trying. Don't give up. Oh, Excellent! What's another message, do you think?
Child:	They are prisoners.
Teacher:	That the chickens are prisoners! What else, Ted?
Ted:	That the chickens want to get free.
Teacher:	To free the chickens. Do you think that's why they made the movie – to try to make you think about chickens that are in captivity?
Child:	Don't lock chickens up.

In this teacher–student dialogue, the class was prompted to consider the intentions and interests of the designers of *Chicken Run*. Interestingly, Ted interpreted a key message of the movie as one of developing perseverance – 'Not to stop trying'. The teacher readily accepted this as one among multiple possible interpretations of the text. It was Ted who supplied an alternative possible meaning of the text: 'That the chickens [in captivity] want to get free'. In the absence of the teacher's questioning, the learners would not have examined the underlying message about animal captivity, nor recognised the way they were positioned as viewers to empathise with their feathered friends in *Chicken Run*.

The learners gained access to designs of meaning by considering the message of the text ('What is the message that the movie creators are trying to get across to you?'). They were guided to think about whose point of view or perspective was represented ('That the chickens are prisoners' who 'want to get free'). They examined whose interests were served, and the social and environmental choices associated with poultry farming ('Are there chicken farms where children are allowed to run free?').

It was evident in this and other lessons that the teacher did not regard literacy as an independent variable. Rather, she regarded it as inseparable from social practices, contextualised in certain political, economical, historical and ecological contexts. These students were guided to consider how designs of meaning are culturally specific, serving particular social and environmental ends.

Learners were frequently encouraged to stand back from their own design choices, considering their multimodal texts critically in relation to both forms of analysis. For example, the teacher assisted the following groups of students to functionally analyse the visual and audio design elements of their movies in relation to the intended message and audience – their preparatory buddies.

Teacher: Who's going to be looking at this?
Harry: We've got prep buddies.
Teacher: So do they know that this is a spoiler and that that's the exhaust? Do you understand what I'm trying to encourage you to think?

[Later]

Teacher: Are you happy with that?
Girls: [nod]
Teacher: Are you sure? Do you think people would understand what you are saying, because remember, this is playing when your photos are coming up slowly at the end. So do you need to speak so quickly?

The teacher encouraged the students to consider the relationship between the duration of the audio text and the moving visual images, so that the two modes were combined effectively. In this way, critical framing was closely linked to transformed practice, and critical framing became grounded in everyday social purposes.

A decisive intellectual shift occurred when students began to analyse their own movies independently of the teacher. For example, the four boys who made '*Slip, Slop, Slap*' analysed the clarity of the visual elements of their storyboard in relation to their social purpose.

Jack: What's that coming out of the shore?
Matthew: Why don't we make that an illusion of something frightening, but it's just a big rock?
Jack: What do you think?
Nick: I'm thinking, I don't think the prep kids would understand that.
Jack: Oh yeah!
Matthew: Good point.
Mark: Yeah, good point [laughs].

Nick, as an expert novice, focused the group's attention on analysing how everyday designs of meaning and discourses work to communicate certain interests for particular audiences and cultural purposes (e.g. 'I don't think the prep kids would understand that'). The teacher's consistent modelling of critical processes had empowered these learners to analyse independently how their own multimodal designs situate readers.

Critical framing was an important strength of the teacher's enactment of the multiliteracies pedagogy, and this had significant consequences in terms of the students' empowerment to access designs of meaning for themselves. The observed pedagogy realised Kalantzis and Cope's (2005) ideals for the enactment of critical framing, because the learners were able to use the two thinking processes described at the outset of this section – to analyse texts both 'functionally' and 'critically'.

The students were able to understand the general functions or purposes of texts, once explained to them, and made connections between design elements, such as gestures, camera angles and sound effects in relation to the message of the text. More importantly, these learners were beginning to critically analyse the underlying human intentions and interests of the authors and producers, which drives the consumption of multimodal texts in children's everyday world of textual experiences, from book to screen. They were encouraged to consider multiple readings of texts and alternate points of view rather unlocking or reproducing the 'correct meaning'.

Extending this, students were beginning to combine both forms of analysis – critical and functional – to the cultural purposes and meanings of their own designs, grounded in everyday social purposes. It resulted in a powerful and necessary pedagogy that equips students with the skills to contest the pervasive consumer culture characteristic of the new times (Kalantzis & Cope, 2005).

As teachers around the world enact the multiliteracies pedagogy in their local contexts, it is hoped that they can experience the deep satisfaction of seeing students engage more consciously in critical and reflective learning, while designing multimodal texts for real and varied cultural purposes.

Transformed Practice

Joseph: Then put a speech bubble up from the mum's head like, 'What are you doing? The car's not stopping!'
David: 'Look, you're supposed to look right, then left'.
Rose: Like, 'You're meant to look right, and left and right'.
Joseph: Look twice: then you can cross!

Here, three students negotiate the linguistic elements of their movie – *Crossing the Road* – to complement the moving images. The planned image sequence would show a mother and a child waiting at the curb for a rapidly approaching car. They would either use speech balloons on cardboard signs or recorded voice-over to clarify the action in the narrative.

The children built upon one another's verbal contributions as they collaboratively modified, extended and refined the text to communicate their intended message to the preparatory buddies. The students engaged in transformed practice as they redesigned meaning, transferring their ideas from one cultural situation – a television road safety campaign – to their own social context and purpose.

This section describes the transformed practice that was evident both in the processes and product of claymation movie making. Transformed practice is the climax of the multiliteracies pedagogy. This is because transformation occurs when students demonstrate that they can transfer their knowledge to work successfully in new contexts (Kalantzis & Cope, 2008). Rather than focusing on the teacher's actions, there is a greater emphasis here on evaluating the effectiveness of the students' designs. I evaluate the degree to which the students' movies demonstrate the 'application' of knowledge and skills 'creatively' and 'appropriately' (Kalantzis & Cope, 2008: 185–186).

What counts as transformed practice in a pedagogy of multiliteracies? For example, what if the students followed a set of procedures in a keyboarding tutorial, copied sentences neatly from the blackboard, or retold a story using correct grammar and orthography? In fact, none of these literacy tasks constitute transformed practice. This is because they purely involve applying knowledge appropriately – good reproduction of conventions – rather than requiring a significant level of creativity and innovation. A requirement of transformed practice is that learners transfer meaning-making practice by putting meaning to work in other contexts or cultural sites, such as the original movie making that occurred in this research (New London Group, 2000).

The teacher created a learning environment in which the six groups of students could choose a unique educational movie theme. They could potentially utilise unlimited combinations of semiotic resources, materials and technologies to communicate a message, driven by their own interests, to a real audience. The right conditions were established to allow transformed practice to occur.

Matthew, Jack, Nick and Mark, introduced at the beginning of the book, were part of a group of eight students in the class identified as having close to average literacy ability, based on the Queensland Year 5 Tests in Aspects of Literacy (Queensland Studies Authority, 2007b). Their movie – *Slip, Slop, Slap* – transformed meanings from a well-known Australian skin-cancer television campaign to work in another social context.

Researcher:	Is he [plasticine figure] the main character?
Jack:	He's like, the one that comes up and gets sunburned while bathing.
Researcher:	While bathing?
Nick:	Yeah. This is the dude that gets sunburned, but this is before he does.
Matthew:	Yeah, this is the original colour before he's tanned [red plasticine will be used for the character once sunburned].
Teacher:	Now, have you thought about all your characters?
Jack:	Yeah.
Teacher:	What about your sunscreen person – your sunscreen bottle? What are you going to do with that?
Jack:	Oh yeah.
Teacher:	You need it because it's part of your script.

The final movie had three scenes – beach, underwater diving and return to the beach. The main character and central problem are introduced in the first scene, in which a man announced that he was burned from too much sun exposure. In the second scene, he is depicted diving underwater with tropical reef fish to soothe the burns. Jazz music without dialogue provides a relaxing audio background. The final scene returns to the beach where the central problem is still unresolved. An animated sunscreen bottle offers sun protection to the man, squirting him with the liquid. To represent this event, close-up shots of the man's face are shown before and after the sunscreen application. The voiceover warns viewers to *Slip, Slop, Slap,* and a short segment of jazz music concludes the movie effectively.

The most advanced feature of the movie was the audio design, which synthesised scripted dialogue and background music in a sophisticated manner. Conversely, the quality of the visual and spatial elements was limited to some degree by two- rather than three-dimensional representations. However, the boys' application of digital film making knowledge and skills was above average.

The movie was characterised by intertextuality, since the boys transferred knowledge about the health risks of sun exposure without UV protection to the context of a claymation movie for preparatory level students. The message of the movie and the simple plot were highly suitable for the medium of a short animated film for young Queenslanders.

Of the six collaborative groups, these boys required the lowest degree of teacher assistance, while sustaining equal contributions of the four group members. These boys demonstrated an ability to independently apply knowledge appropriately and creatively across different modes of communication.

Four girls, in the average ability group, designed *The Case of the Disappearing Pimples.* The group included Sarah and Elizabeth, Anglo-Australians, and Emma, of Maori descent. Meliame, the Tongan student introduced in Chapter 1, was also a group member. These girls employed intertextuality by making connections to a popular 'reality television' program. In this way, a cross-cultural aspect of meaning-making was evident in this transformation. The opening scene was a party in a beautifully decorated room, where the central problem – pimples from junk food – was introduced. The setting shifted to a close-up of the main character's face, and the technique of lip synchronising was used during the dialogue.

The second main scene was a shopping centre where three of the characters purchased fresh fruit and vegetables, and skin products. Two weeks later the girls were eating healthy sandwiches and were complementing the main character about her clear skin. The audio elements alternated between carefully scripted dialogue, narration and party music that precisely matched the duration of the images. The teacher described the movie sound as 'excellent'.

The message of the text was communicated implicitly in the plot and explicitly in the final voice-over and complementary text: 'Don't eat too much junk food'. An interesting caveat is that the movie theme – pimples – was somewhat removed from the experiences of their intended preparatory audience, and would be understood only by the audience on parent night.

This hybrid, multimodal text was characterised by a significant degree of transformed meanings and originality, particularly the visual, audio and filmic techniques applied. Sarah had demonstrated the greatest degree of initiative during the movie-making process. She expertly apprenticed Meliame to share the technical roles of filming and creating animations. The movie was more complex than those produced by the other groups, doubling the number of animations, varying the camera angles, and including a more sophisticated script. The pedagogic outcome was more than an exact replication or precise reproduction. The movie design had required transferring ideas from one context and modifying them to produce imaginative originality and generative hybridity (Kalantzis & Cope, 2000a).

The Healthy Picnic was a movie designed by four students of mixed ethnicity from the low literacy ability group – Daria, Joshua and Ted, described in Chapter 1, and Julia, a new student at the school, who was Anglo-Australian.

The establishing scene was a long shot of a suburban park teeming with animations of insects, birds and people to create the background rhythms of life. The setting shifted to a close-up scene of a chequered picnic tablecloth taken from aerial perspective, demonstrating the assembly of a salad sandwich using real ingredients. While the students could draw from an infinite range of possible movie plots and themes, this group drew largely upon one of the teacher's examples to the whole class:

> So take my healthy sandwich idea: if you are going to have a healthy sandwich, your first box [in the storyboard] might be an empty plate. Your next scene might be bread moving onto the screen to sit on the plate. Then you might have a piece of ham, cheese, lettuce, tomato, then on the top, the other piece of bread. Then you might have a bite taken out the sandwich until the sandwich is completely gone with some crumbs on the plate.

The group chose to represent these ideas closely, but still had the significantly challenging design task of representing these ideas through new and unfamiliar modes and media. For example, they used the resource of a scalloped cookie-cutter between photos to remove neat, bite-shaped pieces of the sandwich, until only crumbs remained. The movie climaxed with a plasticine ant consuming the crumbs. The group chose to use background music rather than scripted narration or dialogue, which complemented the moving images very effectively. When asked to explain the message of the text, the students provided a twofold response: (a) 'To eat healthy food'; and (b) 'How to make a healthy sandwich'.

This movie involved a significant measure of transformation rather than an exact replication or precise reproduction of an existing design. These learners drew upon the existing ideas provided by the teacher, yet reinvented or revoiced meanings in a way that had never occurred in exactly the same manner before. The movie demonstrated a high level of aesthetic appeal and charm, with a clear message that centred on a current issue of national priority in Australia – childhood health and obesity. These cultural meanings were appropriately communicated to their preparatory audience through a unique combination of multiple modes of meaning (e.g. visual, audio, spatial, gestural and linguistic). Close reproduction was not the aim or outcome of designing.

David, Joseph, Rose and Paweni were also in the low-literacy-ability group. Their movie *Crossing the Road* climaxed with a car colliding with the child, who was immediately rushed to a nearby hospital in an ambulance.

Rose: Ah, title of the claymation? [Reading from a worksheet]

David: Do you want to, um, do, um, 'Look out, look out – there are children about?'

Joseph: You mean, 'Watch out, watch out – there's danger about?'

David: 'Look out, look out – there's children about', like …

Rose: 'cause that's really good for our buddies.

The teacher had suggested to the whole class: 'You might want to choose crossing the road safely – look left, look right, look left again, hold an adult's hand'. These learners made an intertextual connection between the teacher's suggestion and a familiar television road safety slogan, 'Look out, look out, there are children about'. This educational theme was highly appropriate for their preparatory buddies and the parent community, and the plot was simple, but effective for the intended audience.

The visual and spatial design elements of the movie were limited by lack of attention to detail. For instance, the wooden characters still had hardened pieces of plasticine from previous groups mingled with the new colours. The lines on the movie set depicting a built environment were not measured or ruled. There was a general lack of symmetry, perspective and form in the visual composition. During filming, the group required high levels of scaffolding by the teacher. The final movie did not demonstrate that these ethnically diverse students had attained a 'collaborative level of competence'; that is, the students did not become experts of the convention of movie making to a level of becoming 'fully fledged members of a new community of practice' (Kalantzis & Cope, 2005: 96).

The Garage was a movie designed by an ethnically diverse group of four boys from the low-literacy-ability group. Group members included Harry, John and Daniel, who are Anglo-Australians, and Wooraba, who is Indigenous Australian. In the transcript below, two of the boys described the plot of their movie, which included only one scene. Wooraba and John were absent.

Harry: We're just doing The Garage ...

Daniel: It's like, we're making a car [step-by-step], and then someone comes and drives it along and crashed it.

Harry: Into a pole.

Daniel: Into a pole. We don't have to see the crash. We're just like ...

Harry: We're just going to have a wheel coming back and then, boom!

Researcher: And what's the message of the movie?

Daniel: Don't drive too fast!

The movie drew upon a suggestion by the teacher; so again, a degree of reproduction was demonstrated in this movie theme and plot.

Teacher: These are just ideas. You might want to do a car – one about a car being built from nothing to anything. You can have the wheels coming, and the body coming, and then something else, and then making the car, and then the car zooming off with black smoke.

The visual quality of the movie was limited by an over-reliance upon two-dimensional representations in the set, character and prop designs. Of the groups who completed their designs, these boys demonstrated the least effective use of claymation media, tools and conventions, while needing a large degree of teacher assistance. The depiction of mechanics in a garage provides a glimpse of the interests and prior experiences of these working class boys. However, the message of the movie – 'Don't drive too fast!' – had limited application to the lives of their viewing audience, the preparatory buddies.

The sixth movie was *Breaking the News* designed by a group of three Anglo-Australian boys from low socioeconomic backgrounds – Simon, Ben and Tim. They intended to design a TV news report, choosing the theme from one of the teacher's suggestions: 'We've done natural disasters last term – a tornado or a cyclone, an earthquake. One of those might be something you're interested in'.

As described in Chapter 2, these boys required high levels of explicit scaffolding and instruction during the storyboard stage of preproduction.

The complex storyboard, which was to have lengthy narration, followed the generic structure of a television news report. The frames consisted of alternating shots of the journalist in the studio, and live footage of three natural disasters. Because the movie was never completed, this group was unable to reach what Kalantzis and Cope (2005: 95–96) describe as the lowest level of performance, termed 'assisted competence'. This is because they were unable to combine several conventional forms of communication in a meaningful way, even in a structured learning environment.

In essence, the teacher's enactment of transformed practice in the multiliteracies pedagogy engaged the divergent lifeworlds of students with markedly different outcomes. The movies ranged from discernable reproduction to substantial innovation, while the students required dramatically different levels of teacher assistance. It should be acknowledged that the aim of transformed practice – to transfer and juxtapose meanings to work in new cultural sites – was achieved by five of the six groups (New London Group, 2000). The redesigned, multimodal texts provided evidence of the ways in which the learners' active intervention in the world – multimodal designing – also transformed the designers to varying degrees (Kalantzis & Cope, 2000a).

At a deeper level of explanation, the transition from the learners' lifeworlds to claymation designing caused a difficult dialogue between the culture of the institution and the subjectively lived experiences of some students. Certain students, such as the *Breaking News* group, had a greater distance to travel because of the degree of mismatch between their worlds of everyday lived experience and the requisite knowledge and skills of multimodal designing. The prior language experiences that certain students brought to the classroom did not always assist them when they encountered new, digitally mediated modes of communication. More pointedly, transformation occurred easily for the dominant students in an immersion environment in which collaborative designing involved minimal teacher direction.

In contrast, the students from the low-ability group relied more closely on directions from the teacher. Essentially, the degree of transformation demonstrated in the students' multimodal designing paralleled their degree of familiarity with the dominant culture. These findings are supported by Delpit (1988), who observed that children who are not of the dominant, middle-class culture require more explicit teaching methods than those who have spent their lives immersed in the dominant culture and forms of communication.

These conclusions are not disparaging when we remember the words of Lev Vygotsky (1962: 87), 'What a child can do today in cooperation, tomorrow he will be able to do on his own'. For students who have a greater distance to traverse in the journey of learning, we must allow more time, provide more signposts, and become their travelling companions.

Transformed Identities

Media production climaxed with a glamorous Clogie's Award Night – an intertextual reference to the Australian television Logie Awards. Jennifer distributed the awards equitably among the five claymation groups, choosing the multimodal design strengths of each movie, from script to audio design.

MC 1:	And now, the moment you have all been waiting in anticipation for! Welcome to the School Annual Clogie Awards – that's a Logie for clay animation – Clogie. I welcome students, parents and our special guests to our very special presentation of our clay animation awards.
MC 2:	It is great to be here on this exciting night. The next category is very special because the students voted for their most popular movie. The category for this award is People's Choice. The shortlisted nominees for the award are The Garage and The Healthy Picnic [Clapping].
MC 1:	And the winner of the People's Choice award is The Healthy Picnic. [Sound of clapping. The students stride down a red carpet to receive their awards, accompanied by upbeat music].
MC 2:	The final award given tonight is the Gold Clogie award. This award is judged on the basis of how much extra effort the group put into their project. All movies were short listed for this category. Good luck. Drum roll please. The Gold Clogie is: [Opens envelope] The Case of the Disappearing Pimples [Clapping. Dramatic electric guitar music plays]
Elizabeth:	Our group would like to thank Mrs Taylor for believing in our group. Thank you. [Sound of clapping]

The most profound outcome of the media-based lessons was that the students' identities were transformed. Sign-makers not only make new meanings, but also remake themselves through their engagement with others (Kress, 2000a). By taking on situated identities, including the discourses or 'identity kit' of producers, filmmakers and celebrities, the students realised their potential for designing with new confidence (Gee, 1996).

The teacher had a momentous challenge to engage with unique identities of individuals, recruiting these as a resource for learning to unlock the gate of possibility for improved access (Cope & Kalantzis, 1997). She worked towards connecting the pathways of 23 learners across seven ethnic communities, negotiating multiple 'Englishes', the students' diverse economic conditions, and their differing life-world experiences. This challenge was heightened by the newness of the multiliteracies pedagogy in schools, which the teacher had only begun to implement the previous year.

The teacher initiated a pedagogy that differed to Western models of literacy instruction that are dominated by writing with a pencil and paper (or chalk on a blackboard). Instead, she created a learning ecology in which the value of visual, spatial, gestural, audio and linguistic designing was given significantly greater credence. The process of designing claymation movies reflected the purposeful uses of literacy, mediated by new tools and technologies that are ubiquitous in workplaces, communities and daily life outside of school (New London Group, 2000).

A teaching–learning relationship was established that successfully highlighted the functioning of a learning community. For example, students engaged in productive peer-group activities and relationships that centred on the collaborative designing of claymation movies, rather than an exclusively 'expert to novice' transmission of knowledge from the teacher as the only source of informational authority. While at times, collaboration proved unproductive, such as the boys who did not complete their television news report, most groups were productively engaged in meaningful tasks that led to a significant degree of transformation of both the resources and the learners.

In the difficult translation of pedagogical theory to teachers' praxis, studies that provide explicit and honest documentation of teachers' work in classrooms, particularly where cultural and linguistic differences between the learners abound, remain scarce. This chapter has provided a glimpse of how students from overlapping ethnic and socioeconomic backgrounds can participate meaningfully in the authentic social practices and collaborative relationships required for transformed designing that will count for success in the imminent future.

Chapter 4
Multimodality, Media and Access

Teacher:	Now in almost all of your writing I have seen you doing things like this: 'I had "a" apple for lunch'. Ted – I hope you are watching. You do this: 'Can I have "a" apple for lunch?' It doesn't even sound right, does it? So you have to try to remember your rule for 'a' and 'an'. What if the word was 'dog'? 'I have "an" dog for a pet' or 'I have 'a' dog for a pet?'
Children:	'a'
Teacher:	'A dog for a pet'.

This interaction occurred in a grammar lesson taught to 15 students in the low-ability English stream, who received differentiated instruction on the basis of state literacy test scores. Direct instruction was the pedagogy used to explicitly teach this grammar rule, using a conventional display of example sentences on the blackboard, followed by a writing task in which students selected the correct word 'a' or 'an' to be recorded in their copybooks.

The teacher drew attention to the way in which Ted did not use the Standard English rule in his dialect. While Australia is a multicultural society, English is the National language used, taught and tested in primary schools Nationwide (MCEECDYA, 2009). By default, students from minority ethnic communities are positioned marginally with regard to literacy learning and its associated social goods. Students like Paweni (Thai), Daria (Sudanese), Meliame (Tongan) and Ted (Indigenous Australian), with their wide-ranging social histories and language experiences, had a far greater distance to traverse in order to 'catch up' with their Anglo-Australian peers.

This chapter investigates the patterns of advantage and disadvantage in relation to accessing meaning-making through different modes and media in the multiliteracies classroom. Intuitively, one might expect that multimodal approaches to literacy would be more equitable than monomodal approaches, because students can draw from a broader range of resources for making meaning (Thesen, 2001). It also seems plausible that using new digital technologies for multimedia authorship would be intrinsically more motivating for students than conventional writing using pencils. In practice, however, the potentials of multimodal literacies and new digital media to provide greater access to literacy learning cannot be assumed.

While in theory, widening the semiotic landscape to include multi-modal design may open new meaning potentials for certain students, I demonstrate here, and elsewhere in this book, how the dynamics and mechanisms of access and exclusion in relation to multiliteracies are not theoretically neat or elegant. Rather, there are numerous interactions between multiple mechanisms of access, with certain factors being weaker or stronger than others at different times.

Multimodality and Access

In this section, I demonstrate how combining words with other modes became an important cultural resource for meaning-making, particularly for students who were not monolingual speakers of English. One of the key arguments of the New London Group (2000) is the need for literacy curricula to include a broadened repertoire of meaning-making systems across multiple modes.

The term 'multimodal' describes the complexity and interrelationship of more than one mode of meaning, combining linguistic, visual, auditory, gestural or spatial modes. The New London Group (1996) posited these five categories of modes or design elements as a starting point for the development of new 'grammars' or a 'metalanguage' for a broader range of textual elements than linguistics (written words) alone. Multimodal design differs from independent modes because it interconnects the other modes in dynamic relationships (Kress, 2000b).

The New London Group does not argue that multimodal design is entirely new. Multimodal texts have long existed in the form of picture books, magazines, advertising, television, food packaging and so forth. The point is that it has become more pervasive and ubiquitous with the availability of digital technologies. I begin by evaluating the degree to which students were able to draw upon the visual mode in the context of claymation movie making.

During the initial brainstorming of ideas for their movies in small groups, Paweni, a recently immigrated Thai, was initially unable to make any significant verbal contributions because of her limited experience with spoken English. The students in her group discussed the movie plot, which climaxed with a child running ahead of the parent and consequently, being struck by a car.

David: The car should … He [the child] should be on top of the car –
Rose: Yeah.
David: … on the windshield of the car. I'll draw the car.
Joseph: I'll draw the car this time.
Rose: You can have a turn.
Joseph: [to Paweni] Is that what you want? Is this what you want to have? Is this what you want to happen?
Paweni: Yes [nodding].
Joseph: Yeah? Good!

Joseph demonstrated cultural inclusiveness as he invited Paweni to comment on the group's intentions for the design. Joseph asked Paweni a closed question that required an affirmative or negative response, comprehensible to a newcomer of the discourse. He gradually repeated his question, each time extending the phrase, as parents do with young children: 'Is that what you want?' became 'Is this what you want to have?' and similarly, 'Is this what you want to happen?' Supported by the visual images on the backdrop, Paweni was able to nod and respond verbally, 'Yes'.

While Paweni was not yet confident enough to express alternative paths for designing, interactions such as these paved the way for her increased contributions to the design as movie making progressed. Paweni, a newcomer to the dominant culture, became socialised by her peers, into full participation in the activities, artefacts, and knowledge – the sociocultural practices – of the multiliteracies classroom. Paweni's peers soon recognised her ability to represent ideas visually through drawing.

Joseph: Ah, now a pencil. She's a pretty good drawer! [Joseph watches Paweni as she begins to draw trees on the movie background with Rose.]

Paweni had sufficient understanding of spoken English to contribute to the group's intentions for the design. Paweni increasingly initiated such contributions to the visual elements of the backdrop.

Researcher: Are you going to have clouds …?
Rose: I know what we could do. We could make the clouds out of these [cotton wool balls].

David: Why don't we just paint them? We're going to use the wool
               [painted green] for trees.
Joseph: Look – she's doing that. Look [Loud]. Look what's Paweni's
               doing! [Louder]

Paweni was drawing the outline of the clouds using pencil on the background. Paweni was able to independently and expertly translate their ideas, expressed through spoken English, into graphic representations of clouds. She was able to use the visual elements of the movie backdrop as an external reference to support her understanding of speech. The task required students to share meaning using graphic depiction, supported by speech and gestures. This combinatorial use of modes – speech and image – increases the capacity to manipulate and organise ideas through parallel processes.

Combining visual and written modes provides students with the opportunity for creating 'intratextuality' or multimodal relations within the text. For example, Joshua, who was from a low-socioeconomic background, took every opportunity to draw illustrations to accompany his written work. His older sister had taught him how to use simple drawing software, which he practised in his leisure time. Similarly, Matthew was considered an expert cartoonist:

Jack: Matthew, can you get a pencil – you're the drawer.
            He's a better drawer than most of us.
Nick: Yeah – he's like the crazy one!
Mark: He's like, a good drawer.

Storyboarding provided Matthew with an opportunity to contribute his specialist expertise in combining words and images, as he drew a series of images with captions to record the group's ideas for the movie. Combining linguistic with visual, gestural and spatial modes of design gave these students greater agency for communicating than lessons that relied exclusively on print.

Other students benefited from multimodal designing that involved combining words with multiple modes of design.

Sarah: What are we going to do? [For our movie]
Emma: I think we should do healthy food.
Elizabeth: No!
Sarah: Just write it down. [Hands blank storyboard frames to
                Elizabeth]
Meliame: School rules?

Emma:	I don't like school rules. I reckon we could have healthy food and milk.
Sarah:	Write it down – healthy food – whatever. Here ... merely suggestions. [Takes paper from Elizabeth who is not writing, and records the group's first idea] I think ours should be a person. [Begins to draw first frame]
Meliame:	Yes – trying makeup, or something!
Emma:	Don't always talk about make-up – it's too girly!
Sarah:	Why don't we do it about, like a person, and he wants to choose what to eat. And he wants to be healthy – like that [Starts drawing]. Like he has to choose from a pizza ...
Emma:	Oh, that's good!
Sarah:	Or, what was it again, that's right, a sandwich. Sandwich [says slowly, as she writes] and he like, has to get all the materials out and he has to choose [pause].
Elizabeth:	What about someone who gets lots of pimples from eating unhealthy food?
Emma:	That's disgusting! [The girl's faces show disgust]
Girls:	[Laughter]
Sarah:	Why don't we list a few rude ideas?
Meliame:	Why don't we just get some dots? [Gesturing drawing dots with pencil]
Elizabeth:	No, use play doh – cool!

The preproduction stage of movie making began with developing the movie concept, represented as a storyboard. A storyboard is a series of picture frames for each movie scene, with accompanying labels or a script. The girls considered delivering a message to the school community about developing healthy food choices. The movies would be screened for parents and siblings at a Clogie Awards night – a pun on the Australian TV Awards – Logies.

Jennifer had recently taught the text structure of story narratives, assisting the students to transfer knowledge of written text structures to movie designing. As the girls spoke, they created a series of two-dimensional, simple drawings in four scenes. Later, they planned audio elements to complement the images in each scene, including music, dialogue and voice-over (see Table 4.1).

An outcome of transformed practice in multiliteracies is the original generation of a hybrid text, or original text form, with a specific cultural purpose and audience (Fairclough, 2000). In contrast to the grammar lesson cited at the beginning of this chapter, movie making allowed

Table 4.1 Audio: Dialogue for the case of the disappearing pimples

Scene 1 – Party	'Let's party and dance!' [Jazz piano music]
Insert – Close-up	'Oh, I've eaten too much fatty food'.
Scene 2 – Shops	(1) 'I'm getting pimples from eating too much junk food'. (2) 'Let's buy some healthy food'. (3) 'How about some fruit?' (4) 'Look, some Clearasil' (5) 'This should get rid of my pimples'.
Scene 3 – Eating healthy food	'Guess what? My pimples have gone!' 'Yeah, you look pretty'. 'Thanks'.
Insert – Close-up	'Yum, this healthy food is delicious'.
Coda – Girls hold up written words on cardboard signs to reinforce movie message	[Voice-over] 'Don't eat too much junk food!'

transformed practice to occur because there was the possibility for com-mitment of the producers to the message. There was a greater sense of modality, because the meaning-making was not predetermined. The writ-ten component of the task did not limit what learners could contribute of themselves and their life-world experiences.

In the grammar lesson, the semantic elements of the task were restricted so tightly that the learners' designs lacked a diversity of meaning-making and limited the creative transformation of available resources. Kalantzis and Cope (2005) make an important distinction between applying appro-priately, which is the correct application of knowledge in a specific situa-tion, and applying creatively, which is the innovative application of knowledge, or transfer to different situations. Both elements are impor-tant in transformed practice.

The students' movie scripts were not simply reproductions of linguis-tic conventions. They were driven by a genuine social purpose for the designs – to communicate an educational message to members of the school community. They constituted literacy practices that are similar to those used in social contexts beyond the school. Importance was not attached to learning English at the lexico-grammatical level alone, at the expense of other modes.

Media and Access

Knowing the affordances and constraints of the new media and technologies for representation had a significant influence on students' access to multimodal designing. This was most apparent when digital tools for designing were introduced for the first time. In claymation movie making, stop-motion animation techniques are applied by digitally shooting the characters and other moving objects one frame at a time. Movie animators are required to manually reposition objects slightly between each frame to create the illusion of life-like motion.

The affordances of stop-motion animation techniques are not easily perceived without specialist knowledge of the filmic medium. I use the term 'affordances', following Gaver (1991), as properties that are compatible with and relevant for people's interactions. When affordances are perceptible, they offer a direct link between senses and potential action; hidden or false affordances may lead to mistakes. Different media have different abilities to reveal affordances, by reason of their inherent design (Gaver, 1991). To illustrate this point, consider how the boys who created the movie *Slip, Slop, Slap* initially struggled to understand how to represent shooting liquid through stop-motion techniques for creating animations.

Nick:	The sunscreen bottle guy's got this flame-thrower thing that … [Completes sentence by gesturing a shooting action with his hands.]
Mark:	A flame-thrower thing?
Jack:	Yeah, the sunscreen bottle, the sunscreen bottle – he's got this little tube thing and he just shoots. And he sprays out sunscreen onto the man!
Nick:	And it's, and it's [Gestures gun shooting with sound effects]
Teacher:	How are you going to film that idea? [Using still image photography – not a video camera]
Nick and Mark:	Don't know.
Matthew:	We could have a little hose cut out of him and a little string, piece of string cut into him!
Nick:	Yeah!
Teacher:	Mmm, that's going to be hard. Mmm.

The boys discussed how they would represent a series of action in which the hero of their movie – an animated sunscreen bottle – would shoot sunscreen to protect the main character from the sun's ultraviolet rays. Having no prior engagement in claymation filmmaking, they did not anticipate the design constraints that would be encountered if they attempted to photograph shooting sunscreen using a series of still images.

The underlying difficulty concerned overcoming the constraints of stop motion techniques for representing their idea of shooting liquid, while the choice of mode (visual) was only backgrounded. A key difficulty was that the students needed to understand the affordances of the technologies and media in order to know and access the design possibilities (Gaver, 1991).

Jack:	Or he's just standing there, and he's like that first [Gestures holding rifle action]. And then he shoots [Makes gunshot sound] and then you just see it.
Mark:	You just see a little bit of sunscreen coming out.
Teacher:	So you're going to have a little bit coming out? How are you going to make it stay though?
Mark:	With a piece of string. Like, just hold it up [Gestures holding something suspended on string].
Jack:	Yeah, you could just, like, get something across, and just tie it there if you want it to stay, or something.
Teacher:	You'll probably need fishing wire then, wouldn't you – that people can't see. If it's real string people are going to see it!
Nick:	[Talking through teacher] Take a photo. Take a photo of something and then put it in.
Jack:	– That'd be pretty hard. No, you just, you like, film it like that [Gesturing rifle action], and then you see where the white thing is.

[Later]

Teacher:	Do they actually have to see the bottle spraying? Maybe you could have a close-up of your character getting sprayed.
Nick, Mark and Matthew:	Yeah!
Jack:	True.
Teacher:	You don't have to have all long shots.
Mark:	Yeah – we could do that!
Jack:	Mmm.
Teacher:	Like the year 2's last year had just all long shots. There's no reason why you can't have a couple of close-up shots with just that character being sprayed.

Mark: Yeah, we should have a close-up of him in the movie!
Jack: Yeah, yeah – let's do that!

The students could not anticipate a way to represent shooting sunscreen to their viewers. It is easy to create the illusion that figures are moving autonomously by constantly repositioning stable plasticine characters on the stage between each still photo. However, representing shooting liquid is an entirely different matter in clay animations, since flying objects, such as birds, are usually suspended by invisible thread to avoid photographing the animators' hands. The teacher guided the students to consider the limited affordances of stop-motion animation techniques for this particular purpose (e.g. 'How are you going to make it stay though?').

Jack's suggestion – 'No, you just, you like, film it like that and then you see where the white thing is' – preempted the idea of using 'before' and 'after' shots. This cinematic technique allows viewers to infer that something has occurred, rather than seeing the details of the action. The teacher elaborated Jack's idea by asking the question, 'Do they actually have to see the bottle spraying?' Through talk, the teacher guided the learners to realise how screen shots can switch between different characters participating in a single interaction.

The teacher then introduced a key affordance of camera angles: 'Maybe you could have a close-up of your character getting sprayed'. Interestingly, the boys had depicted all frames on the storyboard as long shots, continually representing their ideas as whole figures against backgrounds. They did not consider the possibility of representing objects through different shot types. Later the teacher assisted the group to consider the potential of digital cameras to create close-up shots using the zoom function. Close-up shots make possible the selective indication of important details, and can be used to indicate social proximity (Kress & van Leeuwen, 1996).

The notion of affordances is a central factor in explaining the accessibility of new technical interfaces for multimodal design. Technologies and media application have unique combinations of attributes that make possible and apparent, certain actions. Some interfaces have affordances that are more transparent and easy to use than others, by reason of their design (Gaver, 1991). Unlike conventional representation using a pencil, the visibility of the affordances of the mediating technologies for multimodal design was not always apparent.

Access to multimedia authorship required sophisticated knowledge of the affordances and limitations of new digital media for representation, such as technical codes for representing movement in stop-motion films. The students were required to depict an imagined event by attending to visual, spatial and gestural elements of the design. However, it was their limited understanding of the digital media that was most constraining.

This issue became most apparent during filming. The boys stood facing the digital camera, which was mounted on a tripod and angled at the movie set on a desk.

Jack:	Ready? [He takes two photographs. The other boys simultaneously merge toward the movie set to move figures, hands reaching awkwardly.]
Jack:	Right, good! Now, some seagulls. Just move it really, really carefully!
Nick:	That's all right [One bird fell off].
Mark:	Well, one could have flown away!
Nick:	Move the umbrella.
Mark:	No – don't move the umbrella [non-living object]. Put the umbrella down!
Matthew:	No, it's got to be [moved] a little bit. *A little bit!* [Shouting]
Nick:	Oh! This is going to be [Sigh].
Mark:	Ah, where's the other seagull gone?
Matthew:	Ok, don't move them too much!
Jack:	Have you moved everything?
Mark and Nick:	Yes.
Jack:	And the man?
Mark:	We moved him!
Jack:	Can't you move the shells?
Mark:	No – the shells don't move!
Nick:	Matthew! You just moved everything I did, which means they just moved twice!

Certain non-living objects in the boys' movie needed to remain stationary, such as umbrellas, shells and rocks. Nick and Jack did not understand which objects needed to be animated (e.g. 'Move the umbrella!' and 'Can't you move the shell?'), while Mark could identify the living creatures to be moved, but did not explain his reasoning (e.g. 'No – don't move the umbrella', and 'The shells don't move'). The boys shifted the figures in back-and-forth motions, rather than in consistent and purposeful trajectories. This is a common difficulty when designing the temporal axis of a claymation movie.

Filmmakers must visualise how the accumulation of still photos and the repositioning of the objects in each shot will result in specific variables of movement, such as direction, speed and fluidity (Burn & Parker, 2003).

The animation process does not allow users to shift between filming and digital editing – when the effectiveness of the animations can be viewed on the screen. Rather, filming is a process of hypothesis making, in which filmmakers must anticipate, based on prior experience, the final effectiveness of animations on the screen.

This technical constraint of digital designing can be overcome through sustained and repeated engagements in similar movie-making projects. During the introduction of new technologies, even the most competent users were initially unable to perceive the affordances of the filmic medium to represent their ideas. The design of the technology itself was a factor influencing the fluidity with which the students took up digital tools.

Transmediation and Access

In this section, I demonstrate how the shifting of semiotic meanings played a necessary and significant role in the students' take up of multimedia authoring. 'Transmediation' is a term coined by Charles Suhor (1984: 250) to denote the 'translation of content from one sign system into another'. Transmediation deals with the structure of sign systems, and the connections between them for making sense of human experience. Sign systems refer here to the multiple semiotic structures through which humans communicate meaning, such as through writing, digital design, drawing, dance, music or mathematics.

Transmediation concerns more than shifting meanings across the five modes – visual, spatial, gestural, audio and linguistic – as theorists of multiliteracies conceive modes (New London Group, 1996). Rather, it is a syntactic concept that deals with the structure of sign systems and their conventions. When knowledge is expressed through one or more symbol systems and re-expressed in another, this process can facilitate incremental changes to understanding (Suhor, 1984: 247–257).

Transmediation is central to all stages of movie making, from pre- to post-production, because meanings formed in one communication system must be recast in the context and expression planes of a new sign system. For example, students initially represent their ideas through a storyboard – a labelled sequence of still, two-dimensional images. These linguistic and visual meanings are translated into three-dimensional artefacts as movie characters, costumes and props. During movie production, the artifacts are animated and digitally recorded using still image photography.

A written script is translated into permanently recorded dialogue or voice-over using audio recording software. Other symbol systems, such as music and sound effects, can be utilised to enhance, modify or complement the moving images on the screen. Central to the process of transmediation in digital movie making is the ability to shift semiotic content across multiple media applications, such as between sound recording and movie editing software.

To illustrate the central role of transmediation in digital media creation, I focus here on the post-production stage of movie making. The aim was to create the audio elements of the movie – recorded dialogue, sound effects and music – and combine them with the moving images on the screen.

The group of Anglo-Australian boys who created the movie *Slip, Slop, Slap* decided to anticipate how the scripted dialogue, music and images would come together, prior to digitally recording the dialogue using the Sound Recorder interface. Mark and Nick were seated at one computer to play the silent image sequence. Jack was seated at another machine to run the digital music track during the second scene. The boys also practised timing their scripted speech to match the images in the first and third movie scenes.

Mark:	[Plays the third section of the movie images with the music track]
Jack:	This music isn't for the end of the movie [Frustrated tone].
Nick:	This is for the water [Scene].
Mark:	Yeah, I know. I'm just looking to see how our movie is [Images only].
Jack:	All right, let's practise saying it. All right. You ready? Talk Mark! Get it to the start.
Mark:	[Starts playing images] 'Gee, you look sunburned!'
Nick:	[Misses cue for next line of script]
Mark:	[Repeats cue] 'Gee, you look sunburned!'
Nick:	[Misses script cue again]
Jack:	Are you ready? Go Nick! [Now the movie has started and the boys wait for it to finish before playing it back.]
Mark:	[Starts movie again] 'Gee, you look sunburned!'
Nick:	'I'll feel better after a swim'.
Jack:	[Misses cue to start playing the music file for Scene Two]
Mark:	[Starts movie again] 'Gee, you look sunburned!'
Nick:	'I'll feel better after a swim'.
Jack:	[Misses cue for the music file again] I'll add the music first. [Before practising the script].
Jack:	[Plays a music file to match Scene Two of the images on the second computer. The music stops before the images finish]

Mark: Yeah.
Researcher: The music file is not very long, is it?
Jack: We're going to slow it down. Ready, set, go! [Mark plays the moving images as Nick begins rehearsing the script to match Scene One]

In this semiotic process, the boys provisionally combined moving images with a digital music track, while simultaneously attempting to rehearse their scripted dialogue. Appreciably, the boys needed to rehearse their multimodal orchestration numerous times, simultaneously combining differentiated meanings across multiple symbol systems – scripted speech, moving image and instrumental music.

Transmediation involved a search for commonality between sign-making systems, yet the inconsistencies between semiotic codes called for adaption and invention to synthesise meanings. This is demonstrated when the boys consistently miss their cue in this complex synchronisation.

At a critical point in this rehearsal, Jack decided to temporarily omit the speech rehearsal to focus on coordinating the digital images and music ('I'll add the music first'). This was a task already requiring the transmediation of meanings between two sign systems, facilitated by two computers and two media applications for replaying moving images and sound separately. After successfully combining image and music, they reintroduced the rehearsing of speech, shifting meanings between multiple modes simultaneously.

Jack: All right, let's practice saying it. All right, you ready? Get it to the start. Ready, set, go! [Mark plays the moving images on a computer as Nick begins rehearsing the script to match Scene One]
Nick: 'Gee, you look sunburned!'
Mark: 'I'll feel better after a swim'.
Jack: [Uses a second computer to play the jazz music recording to match Scene Two of the moving images]
Mark: 'Ow! That made my sunburn worse!' [Speech timed to match Scene Three]
Nick: 'Here, have some sunscreen'. [The duration of the images and words are equal]
Researcher: Mmm, that fitted quite nicely!

The semiotic process of transmediation was central to this form of multimedia authorship, resulting in the generative creation of an original text. They reconfigured the semiotic resources available to them in the simulation of meanings, to anticipate the final audio-visual text. This temporal synchronisation of meanings was achieved prior to using the digital editing software to combine the discrete digital files as a permanent montage of modes. This process proved essential when they came to digitally edit the movie, because the duration of the dialogue matched the duration of the corresponding movie scenes (see Table 4.2).

This demonstrates that transmediation is fundamental to multimodal and digital design because it requires the recasting of meaning through the context and expression plane of multiple semiotic structures. The multimodality of textual production and use in society today necessitates that students learn to transmediate flexibly between sign systems. Each sign system has unique organisational principles, involving elements and conventions that do not have precisely equivalent meanings (Siegel, 1995: 458).

The potential for generative thinking is heightened as authors and readers make connections between multiple sign systems, given the heterogeneity between sign-systems. The role of digital technologies in transmediation has been little explored in the literature, presenting different sets of possibilities and complexities for shifting meanings across sign systems. A multiliteracies approach allows learners to transmediate meanings across sign systems, which is increasingly important in everyday textual practices in a digital world.

Table 4.2 Movie scenes and audio in *Slip, Slop, Slap*

Scene 1	Scene 2	Scene 3	Scene 4
Location: Beach	Location: Reef	Location: Beach	Location: Film Studio
Action: Main character meets sunscreen man walking along the beach.	Action: Main character scuba diving in the reef.	Action: Main character becomes covered in white plasticine	Action: Still portrait photo of four boys
Sound 1:	Sound 2:	Sound 3:	Sound 4:
Sunscreen Man: 'Gee, you look sunburned!' Sunburned Man: 'I'll feel better after a swim'.	[Jazz music track]	Sunburned Man: 'Ow – that made my sunburn worse!' Sunscreen Bottle: 'Hey dude – have some sunscreen!' [Squirting sound]	Boys in unison: 'Don't forget to Slip, Slop, Slap'.

Agency and Access

While multimodal and multimedia designing opened up new semiotic possibilities, an important caveat is that students exercised differing degrees of agency in utilising these opportunities. What I call a 'dialectic of access' occurred, that is, there was reciprical interaction between the agency of the student, and the socially produced learning structures, including the rules and resources for representation.

Following Giddens (1981), agency is used here to refer to the flow or pattern of human actions, rather than human intentions for doing things. The students' 'take-up' of opportunities for multimodal design in the context of the classroom is conditioned by the existing learning structures, while also producing and reproducing those structures through their action.

Ted:	[Repeatedly clicking a retractor pen against the top of his shoes while Daria draws and labels the storyboard frames]
Joshua:	[Stares at floor. He has not contributed to the group yet, showing sullen facial expressions due to a conflict with peers during the lunch break]
Daria:	[Finishes drawing and passes storyboard to Julia.]
Ted and Joshua:	[Shift positions to lie on their stomachs, watching Julia draw now.]
Ted:	[Laughs and makes inaudible comment to Julia about the drawing]
Julia:	[Smiles and rolls eyes, as if teased. Then looks at Daria and asks a clarifying question about Daria's previous drawings in the frames]
Daria:	Don't forget the salt and pepper.
Julia:	Oh yeah!

The collaborative nature of the movie-making task provided space for the students to draw upon their distributed expertise, rather than locating a full repertoire of knowledge and skills for authorship in the individual. However, the students' action differed in relation to taking hold of, deferring to others, or resisting opportunities provided to them to access specialist multimodal designing.

Jennifer had explicitly addressed the issue of distributing the linguistic and visual aspects of multimedia authorship fairly among students, irrespective of their modal preferences.

Now that does not mean – sitting up, please – that John Jackson, because he is good at art is going to draw *all* of the frames. He might want to draw one of them, but someone else in his group can come up with the other one. All in the group have to work on the script together – it's only fair.

Students were knowledgeable agents in terms of the mutually understood norms and rules for collaborative work, such as taking turns, listening to others, completing work in a timely manner, and so forth. Despite this explicit guidance for the distribution of labour, and having available material resources, not all students routinely contributed to multimodal designing.

I posed questions to these students about their actions whenever there was a lapse or fracture in the general patterns of engagement in movie backdrop design. Some students would gaze blankly, and then walk away, as if having not heard my voice. I asked Meliame: 'Have you got anything to do now?' She tossed a piece of fluff in the air and offered a cheeky smile. Joseph walked past:

Researcher:　'What are you doing Joseph?'
Joseph:　　'Hey? Ah, doing that!'

He pointed to the cardboard car that the support teacher was making, and rested his arms on David's shoulders. The teacher later commented, 'Joseph is having a holiday over there'.

[Ted saunters past].

Student Teacher:　If you're just walking past, see if you can be of help somehow.
Researcher:　　[To Julia seated at the book publishing table.] What are you making?
Julia:　　I'm making a bee [Using plasticine].

[Ted approaches the table, limbs swaying from side to side].

Researcher:　　Why don't you make some insects for the backgrounds? [To Ted]
Julia:　　Ah hum [Agreement with the researcher] There's enough clay there, Ted [She points to the selection of plasticine].

[Minutes later, Ted walks in front of the researcher's camera to attract attention.]

Active contributions to the multimedia authorship were unevenly distributed among group members, with certain roles dominated by some, while actively resisted by others. A recurring pattern became evident in the routinised action of the multiliteracies classroom. Students who were not of the dominant, Anglo-Australian culture, and those from the low-ability English stream were least involved in filming movies using the digital camera. These students frequently resisted, or deferred to others, roles that required technical skills, such as framing the movie composition, varying camera angles and stop-motion animations.

For example, Sarah directed the digital aspects of filming, taking the exclusive role as the photographer over the four-hour filming period. Meliame carried out Sarah's explicit directions for each animation, but avoided using the camera. Emma and Elizabeth initially counted the number of photos taken, but were constantly off-task. During lunch, they chose to play, leaving the other girls to continue filming. When they returned, it was time for the streamed English grammar and writing lessons.

Researcher: Are the other two girls in another class?
Teacher: Yeah, they're in class. There's supposed to be four.
Researcher: Yeah.
Teacher: And ah, Elizabeth and Emma are *very* good at wasting time.
Researcher: Mmm.
Teacher: Those two girls – they're 'professional time wasters'.

The teacher allowed Sarah and Meliame to continue filming during formal English classes to enable them to complete the movie. Her original intention was that all four girls would contribute to movie production ('There's supposed to be four'). The teacher labelled the two off-task girls as 'professional time wasters' – they were experts at subverting classroom norms in ways that were seemingly legitimate.

Sarah: [Arranges the plasticine-on-wood characters on the lounge chair. Emma attaches one plate of food in the hands of a plasticine character. Sarah and Meliame rearrange the rest of the plates neatly on the table.]
Elizabeth: [Standing motionless, gazing into distance, one finger to mouth.]
Emma: Sandwiches! [To Elizabeth]. You can just make sandwiches or little hamburgers [Joining the 'plates' together, which now function as two pieces of bread.]

Sarah:	Hamburgers! Just squash them together. [Sarah walks toward Meliame to make some more together].
Elizabeth and Emma:	[Stand facing one another, chatting, and swinging their arms]
Researcher:	[Prompting Elizabeth and Emma] They're making little sandwiches.
Emma:	Oh, little sandwiches.
Elizabeth:	[Stares at researcher].
Sarah:	Yeah. No, not that way! [To Meliame as she animates the characters on the movie stage]
Elizabeth:	[Stands idle, swaying from side to side]
Sarah:	[Takes two photos]
Emma:	[Records photo] Another one?

When Emma and Elizabeth rejoined the girls, they were newcomers to filming, having failed to gain the same level of situated experience as the girls who were reaching the end of production. Emma took up the role of counting the photographs. Elizabeth actively resisted efforts by the others to contribute to the movie production.

Filming movies required both skilled and unskilled work, from basic counting and recording with a pencil on paper, to sophisticated animation and digital filming techniques. Students who were not of the dominant, Anglo-Australian ethnicity deferred roles that required the use of digital technologies to more expert peers, self-selecting unskilled roles.

David:	Who wants to be the photographer?
Rose:	What's the photographer?
Joseph:	Let Rose be one.
Rose:	I don't want to be – pick Paweni.
Paweni:	No, no!

During filming, Paweni did not venture to touch the digital camera, and had to be constantly reminded by the teacher to move away from certain areas of the filming studio – 'Do not bump the tripod!' and 'Stand back please'. The learning stuctures within the classroom, such as the tacit norms for participation in collaborative group work, the explicit directions from the teacher, and the resources for designing, were not a barrier to the learners' active engagement in multimodal design. Yet the students, through these interactions, reconstituted these structures in different ways. This principle was observed among other groups of students. For example, Julie (Anglo-Australian) was successful in drawing upon the rules, symbols, and resources for designing movie animations and digital filming. This was not the case for Ted (Indigenous) and Daria (Sudanese), who did not draw upon these structures in the same way.

Teacher:	[Arranges the tomato pieces in a square on the bread for the movie]
Julia:	[Takes two photos]
Teacher:	[Moves objects on the movie stage. Her shoes clatter against the floor loudly as she hurries from one side of the movie set to the other, busily arranging objects between shots.] Are you taking these … ah counting these, Ted?
Julia:	[Takes two photos]
Teacher:	[Animates the tomato pieces]
Julia:	Can you smell the tomato? It's wafting this way.
Ted:	[Leans against the classroom furniture, recording the number of photos]
Daria:	[Standing near table]
Julia:	[Takes two photos]
Teacher:	[Moves the 5 pieces of tomato to cover the bread arranged like 5 dots on a dice] Ah hum.
Julia:	[Takes two photos] That's another one, Ted.
Teacher:	[Clears throat. Moves the squares of cheese near the plate] Is that on the screen?
Julia:	Yep
Teacher:	Right. Good. [Teacher animates the cheese].
Julia:	[Takes two photos]
Daria and Ted:	[Standing at side table. Ted removes his jacket and then bangs loudly on the table, as if bored.]
Teacher:	[Moves objects on the set with Julia]
Researcher:	How many photos have they done, Ted?
Ted:	Oh … [Scratches head, walks over to check record and returns too quickly to have read anything]. Ah [Long pause], twenty-five? [Guessing].
Julia:	[Takes two more photos.]
Ted:	[Wandering about looking through the viewfinder at the teacher's back as she animates objects on the set]

Ted complied with the teacher's suggestion to tally the number of photos taken, while acting in ways that demonstrated obvious disinterest. Julia, an Anglo-Australian, took up the most active role in creating animations and using the digital camera, and over the course of the filming session, was effectively socialised into the specialised discourse of film-making. Daria did not have an assigned role, and her occasional participation in creating animations diminished as filming continued.

While claymation movie making provided the opportunity for students to communicate through non-linguistic modes of meaning, a dialectic of agency occurred in which students demonstrated the uneven take-up of the mediating tools for meaning-making.

Society and Access

Teacher: I received a ... letter from [Paweni's] father this morning ... That's the third one I've had from him this year.

Researcher: Really?

Teacher: Saying, 'How dare you give her a project that is way above her! The project you've given her is just way above children at this level. I have questioned her at length and she doesn't understand what to do, and she doesn't even understand what a bibliography is ...' So a really scathing letter – I've given it to Mr Norman [Principal] to deal with.

Researcher: That's terrible – imagine that.

Teacher: I've spoken to him before. But the project ... they've got a choice. They can research an Australian invention and present it as a poster – that's the easy one. That's the one I encouraged her to do, and she didn't want to do it. The other one is inventing a toy, and then filling out the information that you'd need if you wanted to patent it. It's just answering some questions.

Researcher: Right.

Teacher: But the toy could be as simple as making a paper plane.

Researcher: Yeah

Teacher: It could be that simple. Whereas, he thinks I'm talking about inventing a proper, real toy to market in real life and patent in real life.

Researcher: He doesn't realise that it's, that it's a life-like task ...

Teacher: And he says, 'These projects and extra work are just fluffing out the curriculum. And my daughter still can't speak English, so why are you wasting time doing stuff like this'. And I give her so much attention and so much extra time. He forces her at night to copy the dictionary. When I met him, I said something like; 'You don't want to turn her off learning English for life'. But yeah, no, the letter today – my word!

Paweni's father, an elderly Anglo-Australian, who held strong views about the role of schooling, challenged the teacher's decision to include multimedia authorship in the literacy curriculum. According to the teacher's report, he saw creative, multimodal design using digital technologies as 'fluffing out the curriculum'. Teaching formal, written English using traditional pedagogies, such as rote learning of word meanings, was given priority in the home.

This highlights how students' agency to take up multiliteracies in the classroom was influenced by patterns of power and contested meanings in their homes, forming a feedback loop. There was a circular set of casual relations so that a change in one social context influenced another, eventually restoring the social conditions to their original condition (Giddens, 1979).

The differing abilities of students to use multimedia in the classroom were limited by their differing prior experiences with using technology for multimedia authorship at home. Students' unequal degrees of familiarity with the dominant modes and meaning structures (e.g. English) in the society and the school were tied to the students' divergent time–space paths in the local community outside of school. Ethnically marginalised students drew upon different meaning-making resources than those employed in the school. For example, the teacher explained how Paweni, who had arrived in Australia the previous year, drew upon the meaning structures of her Thai language and culture at home.

> Paweni still speaks Thai at home almost full time at home with her mum. Her mum, apparently, according to Dad who's Australian [Anglo], says that mum has come to Australia, but wants desperately to go back to Thailand. She will not give up her Thai culture, and will not speak English. So when Paweni is at home, she speaks Thai to her mum, and when she's at school she speaks English. And that's why I think Paweni is so far behind.

Paweni's lifeworld and home experiences were centred on the meaning structures of her Thai culture, distantly separated from Australian society in time and space. For speakers of the dominant language, drawing upon the structure of English enabled them to achieve their intentions and desires. However, for ethnically and socioeconomically diverse students, like Paweni, Daria and Meliame, the requirement to use English constrained them from expressing their needs at school.

The teacher discussed similar cases of students who spoke different dialects of English.

> If you look at Wooraba, his family is from New Zealand. Their grammar is ... [different] to the way that I'm used to. He writes that way,

and he speaks that way. Mum writes that way and speaks that way, and so does Grandma ... So when I'm conducting writing conferences with him over a piece of work, he cannot pick up ... that it is grammatically incorrect. I try to explain it, but he still doesn't use it, because he writes the way he speaks. That's frustrating for me, but there's not much I can do about it.

Paweni, Daria, Ted, Wooraba and Meliame possessed different linguistic resources to the dominant culture, including dialects of spoken English at home. These students were also marginalised with respect to home computer access. The unintended consequences of these differences in students' home experiences were conditions for the social reproduction of differing access to multiliteracies at school. The students had widely varied structures of action to draw upon, and accordingly, had wholly unequal access in the classroom. The power of students to access multiliteracies in the classroom was partially bounded by the consequences of social action more widely distributed.

Familiarity with the communication structures of the dominant culture played a potent role in either enabling or constraining the students' possibilities for action in the classroom. It demonstrates how students bring to the classroom meaning-making resources that are built up within their worlds of experience in various communities (Luke *et al.*, 2003). The students from diverse cultural backgrounds in this study had been socialised into different multimodal forms of communication, which translated into different kinds of success at school. These relations point toward a pattern in which the conditions for accessing different modes, technologies and media in the classroom were more broadly distributed.

It also demonstrates how any choice of mode, whether word or image, and any choice of medium, whether page or screen, can serve the interests of some, foregrounding certain meanings and silencing others. Multimodal designing via new technologies holds potential for diversifying creativity and increasing the quality and volume of authorial voice and power (Nelson, 2006). However, this chapter has shown that textual practices that draw upon combinations of linguistic, visual, gestural, spatial and audio modes, can be both enabling and constraining for certain students.

Access to multimodal forms of design using new technologies involved a dialectic of access – a dynamic social process, whereby students from varied cultures needed to continually alter their existing conditions of access – such as taking up rules and resources for multimodal designing. Students began with different stocks of knowledge and cultural resources, which they employed with differing levels of transformative capacity within the institutional context of the classroom. A dialectic of access was observed between individual student agency and the available structures of the multiliteracies classroom, which both enabled and constrained students in different ways.

Irrespective of these findings, the importance of broadening the literacy curriculum to include multiliteracies remains unaltered, because the structures for communication in information-based, digitally networked societies now require it. In this study, the teacher provided the students with the opportunity to take the role of filmmakers and producers. Such prestigious forms of knowledge, such as specialist digital movie making, are typically reserved for economically powerful occupational groups (Carspecken, 1996). A multiliteracies approach afforded higher visibility and currency to the cultural themes that were important to the students.

Students should not be denied the opportunity to develop their capabilities with alternate representational forms and technologies, and to combine and translate meanings between modes. Increasingly, students and adults are required to engage with digital media, as knowledgeable, critical and creative consumers and producers.

As designers of new media for their intended audiences, students are positioned to question media convention and messages. To continue to conserve a narrow band of print-based, literary genres, and penmanship skills is to ignore the reality of textual practices in the entertainment industry, the commercial sector, and indeed, the everyday world beyond the school.

Chapter 5

New Social Spaces

In the centre of the studio was an intricate three-dimensional representation of a beach scene, including plasticine figures standing on a sandy shore. The model was illuminated by natural light that entered from the windows, while two lamps were carefully positioned on either side of the model, facing inwards. Directly in front of the model, a tripod supported a digital camera angled slightly downwards towards the display. The class was seated on the carpet behind physical boundary markers around the filming area. The teacher addressed the students:

Teacher: Your floor area will be here. I've got these little signs saying 'Filming in Progress' and 'Quiet Please' there, because this area will be completely out of bounds when filming is happening. I've got a lamp that is going to be turned on here [points to the lamps]. Why? Why do you think I've got a lamp that is going to be turned on here? Rhonda?

Rose: For the light.

Teacher: What about the light?

Rose: So you can see?

Teacher: What do you notice about this light when I'm moving?

Sarah: There's shadows.

David: Shadows

Teacher: There are shadows. Where are the shadows coming from?

Julia: The light through the windows.

Teacher: The light coming through the window is very bright. So to balance that, we need light coming from this direction, because we really don't need your shadows in the movie. So if we had two lamps that are shining this way, then it will give some of your characters depth and dimension. Ok? Lighting is very important.

The dialogue above illustrates how claymation filming involves innovative arrangements of the classroom space associated with new technologies for meaning making. For example, the teacher explained how lighting must be consistent from the beginning to the end of each scene, which can be facilitated by desk lamps to illuminate the movie stage. She explained that the tripod and digital camera must be horizontally and vertically aligned with the set to be filmed.

Floor space is necessary for groups of students to simultaneously shuffle between the movie set and the tripod. New material boundaries must be established to separate new classroom spaces from the old. To a large extent, new tools, media and classroom spaces mediate multimodal designing. In addition, existing components of the classroom are transformed.

I suspect that the majority of tomorrow's classrooms will continue to be physical structures that accommodate people, desks, books and paper. Outside of schools, major cities still bustle with peak-hour traffic as workers transport themselves to the confines of a building, where surveillance and accountability is high, and where productive face-to-face relationships are essential to the well-being of individuals and companies. However, as electronic forms of communication advance in an ever-widening array of hybrid forms, it is imperative that educators, architects and administrators fundamentally rethink how classroom spaces are best arranged to facilitate new ways of learning and representing knowledge.

Historically, the school building has been a corridor separating compartmentalised classrooms in a configuration akin to an egg carton or muffin tray. Classrooms often resemble a theatre, where at best, the teacher performs for sustained periods like an actor before a captive audience, seated in rows. These time-honoured configurations of physical learning spaces are associated with rank, surveillance and teacher-centred pedagogy (Stuebing *et al.*, 1994).

This chapter addresses the relationship between new technologies, classroom space and students' multimodal forms of representation. The findings in this chapter demonstrate that technologies, from pencils to pixels, influence the ways in which learning is mediated (Morgan *et al.*, 2002). In addition, the semiotic or meaning-making potentials of students' multimodal designing both transform, and are transformed by, the use of the classroom space (Jewitt, 2006).

Jennifer envisaged new spaces and places for interactive, collaborative and technology-mediated learning, ultilising the furniture and built environment of the classroom to achieve different learning outcomes. These changes were implemented gradually, with modifications occurring as the need arose. Following Edward Soja (1989), the organisation of the classroom space is a social product, since it arises from purposeful social practice. Social space incorporates social actions, both individual and collective (Lefebvre, 1991). Space is not independent from the wider social framework. Space is not seen here as a separate structure with rules of construction and transformation that are independent from the wider social framework. The organisation and meaning of space is a product of social translation, transformation and experience (Soja, 1989).

Whether it is the form, content and distributional patterns of the built environment, the bodily orientations of the students to learning, or the visual and spatial layout of the screen, all spaces are rooted in social origin, and filled with social meaning (Soja, 1980). Additionally, space and the social organisation of space are dialectically inter-reactive. In other words, social relations of designing are both 'space forming' and 'space contingent' (Soja, 1989: 81). The importance of this work is to understand the semiotic characteristics of multiple modes that are orchestrated in the social production of classroom spaces.

I position classrooms as 'multimodal texts' because classrooms, from traditional to new, are spaces that contain a complex ecology of social actors, discourses, power relationships, cultural artefacts, symbolic systems, architectonic meanings and technologies that form a multimodal composition. A theory of meaning is needed that is broader than linguistics, becuase the spoken and written word have never been exclusive forms of communication in classrooms – nor indeed in social contexts outside of schools (Kress, 2000a).

In this chapter, I describe how Jennifer and her year 6 class utilised modes and media in the context of claymation movie making to socially produce the classroom space as a 'multimodal text'. I use the following categories to analyse socially produced spaces – dialogic, bodily, embodied, architectonic and screen spaces.

Dialogic Spaces

Dialogic spaces for collaboration were the most apparent during storyboard designing. I use the term 'dialogic space' to describe the intertextual and interdiscursive nature of social interactional spaces that are characteristically multi-voiced. The concept draws upon Bakhtin's (1982) notions of dialogic meaning and 'social heteroglossia'. Bakhtin analysed Russian novels, describing how authors speak through the multiple voices of characters. The multiple voices of the characters create a unitary and internally consistent 'dialogic' meaning of the novel.

People, with their various language and frames of reference, construct dialogue to categorise experiences in mutually understood ways.

Dialogisation is more than simply dialogue as speech, because internal dialogisations of many actors occur together to form a unit of meaningful interaction, such as occurred in the classroom. Social heteroglossia is a feature of narratives, but more importantly, of communication between people in social contexts.

I consider here the social interactions that occurred during storyboard design. The transcript below shows some of the multi-voiced dialogue between Jennifer and the students who created the movie *The Healthy Picnic*.

Teacher: So you're all happy with the sandwich idea? Have a sandwich and add fillings, and then it gets eaten?

Ted: [nods] Yeah.

Others: Yeah.

Julia: [nods]

Teacher: And are you just going to take one bite or is the whole sandwich going to get eaten in the end?

Daria: Take one bite.

Julia: No, I was going to have it all being eaten [Loudly, followed by several students talking at once].

Teacher: Yeah, you'll have to make sure, calm down. Now, with the sandwich are you just going to take one bite or have the whole thing eaten by the end of it?

Joshua: Bite, bite, bite and then,

Daria: No, bite, take one bite, take another bite, until it disappears.

Teacher: And there are just crumbs left?

Julia: Yeah.

Joshua: Yeah.

Ted: But how are we going to do the crumbs with plasticine?

Teacher: You can work that out.

Daria: Do, like, balls. [Mimes rolling balls of plasticine]

Joshua: Make them like breadcrumbs.

Julia: Just have a real sandwich!

Ted: Oh yeah, have a real one – I'm eating it!

Daria, Julia, Joshua and Ted communicated their ideas fluidly, building on the contributions of their peers and the teacher to create a movie storyboard. Jennifer revoiced the students' ideas to help summarise the main events ('So you're all happy with the sandwich idea? Have a sandwich and add fillings, and then it gets eaten?').

She shifted the setting to discuss the movie climax ('And are you just going to take one bite or is the whole sandwich going to get eaten in the end?'). This stimulated the construction and deconstruction of ideas and meanings among the students ('Take one bite'; 'No, I was going to have it all being eaten', etc.). She resisted the tendency to inhibit the students' ideas by transmitting her own perspective, and allowed them to arrive at their own consensus.

When the movie conclusion was determined, Ted initiated the next setting or content shift in the dialogue ('But how are we going to do the crumbs with plasticine?'). He was conscious of the need to choose appropriate representational resources to communicate their ideas. Julia enabled the group to realise the richness of materials for claymation designing, which can incorporate combinations of handcrafted, manufactured or natural artefacts (e.g. 'Just have a real sandwich'). The group eventually decided to follow this suggestion; using stop-motion to make the sandwich bread and fillings appear to move by themselves.

In this way, the students incorporated their internal dialogisations into a multi-voiced narrative. When these dialogisations were made available to each other, they became the social heteroglossia of the group (Bakhtin, 1982). Heteroglossia involves dialogic social spaces for multiple perspectives, positioning learners as more than passive listeners.

The storyboard lessons signify an important pedagogical shift for the teacher. For example, earlier literacy lessons had involved the students listening to the teacher's explanations of grammatical rules, and then quietly completing written exercises from the blackboard into their individual writing books. These practices observed in Jennifer's classroom and the school have been traditionally valued in Western classrooms, and can be used effectively. Yet direct instruction of this nature reflects a monologue that closes the internal discourses of the students (Bakhtin, 1982).

Dialogic spaces of authorship were created that shared interactions between the teacher, students and their designs. In this socially produced space, the participants collaborated and reflected on the ideas of others, viewing their peers and the teacher as coparticipants and sources of complementary skills and experiences.

Bodily Spaces

A second kind of social space produced in the movie-making lessons was what I call 'bodily spaces'. These specific 'displays of orientation' include uses of posture, gesture, gaze and other non-verbal modes of communication that demonstrate differing degrees of engagement with curricular artefacts and people (Bezemer, 2008). Bodily bases of meanings are expressed multimodally, frequently accompanying the linguistic elements of speech acts (McNeil, 1992). The concept of bodily social spaces extends the work of theorists such as McLaren (1993) who demonstrated the analysis of bodily postures and gestures as a key to interpreting social relations.

Bodily spaces of meaning were particularly varied during the pre-production stage of movie set and character designing. Three or four lessons aimed to address how to create a movie base, backdrop, and plasticine-on-wood characters. Each lesson was divided into two main lesson frames – short periods of direct instruction followed by time for the students to collaboratively complete their creations. At this stage, the teacher provided tangible examples of movie sets by students from another class. During the lesson introductions, the gaze of the student group was singularly directed at Jennifer as she spoke.

During the collaborative construction time, the students had flexible use of the learning space. They could choose to sit or stand with or without furniture, on the floor, at group tables, or at their desks. The learning space became a non-linear composition, because there were multiple 'reading paths' of the classroom, when seen as a multimodal text (Kress & van Leeuwen, 1996: 220–221).

I use Kress and van Leeuwen's term 'reading paths' – which relates to reading printed texts – as a metaphor for interpreting the social meanings of the classroom as a multimodal text. This is because classrooms are social spaces in which historically, socially and culturally located activities and knowledges can also be 'read' or decoded, being socially produced. Interpreting social spaces implies a process of signification.

Jennifer engaged the children by assisting them to take initiative in self-directed learning. She worked with one group at a time, seated beside the students at at their 'eye level'. This made the teacher and students appear to be 'symbolically equal' (Kress & van Leeuwen, 1996: 116–123). These bodily spaces are significant because it reflected a move away from a hierarchic structure of classroom organisation. There was clearly a more egalitarian, collegial structure wherein the students' ideas were given considerable recognition. The teacher served as a guide, rather than as the sole source of knowledge.

The students' limbs most commonly pointed towards the media, tools and products of the movie-making process. The significance of these bodily orientations is that the students' proxemics – their gaze, posture and tilt of the head towards one another – indicates that they were simultaneously and productively interacting with their peers, while creating the designs in their hands.

An exception to this was when students were off-task, engaged in social interactions with peers that were unrelated to the task at hand. At such times, the students' bodily orientations were singularly directed at their peers, rather than the designs or the mediating tools. In this way, shifts in multimodal displays of orientation were a holistic, bodily demonstration of their level of engagement in the collaborative media work.

Jennifer's goals for the students' learning were significantly more open-ended than in her writing lessons, because movie making allowed the students to take up multidirectional, productive engagements with curricular objects and individuals around them. This contrasts the discourse of direct instruction commonly observed in Western classrooms, which limits the range of accepted bodily displays by the students. For example, during the formal grammar lessons, students were required to orient their bodies to look like listeners, sitting upright, keeping their limbs and hands to themselves and with their gaze primarily concentrated on the teacher.

The bodily spaces of the classroom were significantly transformed during the collaborative multimodal designing of claymation movies. Diverse meanings were created in the multiliteracies classroom, which provided bodily evidence of the learners' collaborative engagement in multimodal designing.

Embodied Spaces

In this section, I use the term 'embodied spaces' to describe socially produced meanings through the material design of artefacts – a multimodal outcome of the students' learning. For example, claymation characters, constructed of various mixed media such as wood, fabric, wool and plasticine, were embodiments of the students' ideas and experiences. Others such as Leander (2002) and Stein (2006) have explored the use of artefacts in the multimodal construction of identities in various classroom settings.

Here, I describe how the students used visual and spatial semiotic resources to reflect plural forms of identification or 'sites of the self' (Holland *et al.*, 1998). Students can construct their sense of identity by producing identity artefacts with multimodal means, projecting new social spaces. For instance, Daria designed a character for her group's movie – *The Healthy Picnic*. There were striking resemblances between Daria's personal and physical markers of identity and those of the figure, such as her Sudanese skin tone, braided long hair and prominent lips.

Similarly, the plasticine costumes of the four girls who created *The Case of the Disappearing Pimples* mirrored their appearance, each with long hair and short skirts. In this way, the girls used visual and spatial resources to reflect and define their own image through the characters, each member contributing elements of their life history and culture (Kress, 2000b).

Therefore, the four girls who created the movie *The Case of the Disappearing Pimples* imagined the characters to be representations of themselves. The following interaction shows how these girls negotiated roles in the movie narrative.

Emma: Or do you want a girl eating lots of chocolate and getting pimples?

Sarah: And then she starts eating healthy food, and the pimples start to go away.

Emma: Meliame can be the girl with the pimples.

Elizabeth: Yeah, because she's not here.

Sarah: No, 'cause she's the boy.

The use of state-of-being verbs in the existential statements 'Meliame can *be* the girl with pimples' and 'she's [she *is*] the boy' demonstrate how the girls were taking on the roles and identities of the characters. Interestingly, they were unwilling to take on personal attributes that were too far removed from their own identities, such as masculinity. In Meliame's absence, the girls allocated to her roles that were least preferred – the female character with pimples and a boy.

The final outcome was an all-female cast of plasticine-on-wood characters, which reflected the gender of their makers. Meliame accepted the unwanted role of the 'girl with the pimples', rather than taking on a masculine role.

In film making, animated characters can be referred to as anthropomorphic agents, embodied agents, or life-like characters (Kipp, 2005). These agents embodied the learners' existing semiotic or cultural resources, including their background experiences with other media. For example, when I asked the girls to tell me about the characters in their movie, the girls reported:

Elizabeth: We're like, the 'Fab Five!'

Sarah: 'Queer Eye'.

The Fab Five is an intertextual reference to the actors in an American reality television series – *Queer Eye for the Straight Guy*, which also screened in Australia. In this program, five gay men do makeovers with the intent to improve heterosexual male grooming habits. The themes of the television program and the girls' movie hinge on the issue of social image. In *The Case of the Disappearing Pimples*, a preteen female becomes self-conscious about an outbreak of pimples the day after eating excessive amounts of 'junk food'. Her peers become her allies, shopping for healthy food and recommending anti-blemish skin products to complete her makeover. When the cosmetic changes take effect, the group celebrates her physical transformation and beauty.

Through the film-making process, the girls transferred the theme of 'image' from the location of popular media culture and its stereotypes, to situate these meanings within their preteen world. Their movie was consistent with the dominant media messages that position females as objects of beauty and eternal youth, rather than as individuals possessing personality, intellect, creativity, spirituality, social and physical abilities and economic or political esteem. Their movie characters embodied cultural connections between TV programs and their preteen worlds. The production of life-like characters made space for an imagined, redesigned world that embodied cross-cultural meanings (Mills, 2010a).

These examples illustrate how multimodal semiotic resources are configured together through tangible designs that embody, shape and reshape identities. The students ultilised representational resources available to them from various cultural contexts. The process of film making mediated their identities in certain ways, restructuring their social relations and experiences. It required taking understandings from one setting and modifying them to reconfigure their identities, media encounters, and social experiences in embodied and multimodal ways. Through aspects of physicality – the weight, size, shape, texture and form of the plasticine figures – they became 'embodiments' of the 'ideas and images in the children's minds', which in turn, were mediated by their media and social environment (Stein, 2006).

Architectonic Spaces

I use the term 'architectonic spaces' to refer to the material qualities of design and structure, which are socially produced. During film making, certain architectonic spaces of the classroom – the spatial arrangements of classroom furniture – were transformed. Prior to filming, Jennifer introduced the function and design of the filming studio. The class sat on the floor opposite the filming space, as she demonstrated with the tripod, camera and movie set. Throughout the lesson, Jennifer invited students to interact with the tools and learning objects. Filming involved the pupils and teacher in bodily interactions with both everyday (e.g. lamps) and cinematic objects (e.g. camera, tripods), which contributed to creating new architectonic spaces.

Movie production – the filming of the movies – occurred in the periphery of the room. This location of the filming area is significant in terms of the 'informational value' of centre and margins in architectonic layouts (Kress & van Leeuwen, 1996: 203). It attested to a dichotomy between Jennifer's goals for multimodal designing and the centrality of formal English lessons (writing) in the school curriculum.

On the one hand, the filming area had subordinate status to the nucleus of information and activity in the centre of the physical space, where students continued to draw upon conventional, print-based media and tools of inscription for the largest proportion of the school day. Conversely, the periphery gained new importance as a specialised and protected space for designing.

The visual framing of the filming area – the spatial boundaries and conjunctions between zones that separated it from other spaces in the room – was significant. Freestanding cardboard signs formed a literal and figurative line along the floor, with the words 'Filming in Progress' emblazoned on a red background. These explicit physical boundaries were established to minimise bodily and noise interferences from other students. A constant camera position and consistent lighting were also required for filming.

These spatial boundaries were reinforced by vacant space around the perimeter, reflecting the status of the filming area as a protected space for specialised digital media work. The filming studio represented what is new, ideal and innovative; yet the existing social structures – the state school curriculum, timetable, and classroom furniture allocations – were historically tied to oral and print-based forms of textual practice.

A central issue here is that the technical requirements of claymation filming required considerably different architectonic spaces – new configurations of the classroom furniture, lighting and built environment – to those required by conventional forms of representation, such as writing on paper and reading with books.

An important feature of the architectonic space during filming was the minimal use of 'partitioning'. Foucault (1977: 143) uses this term to refer to 'allocating individuals to their own space, eliminating groups, and regulating movement'. For example, several boys were allocated isolated desks at the very front of the room. This was a strategic decision by the teacher to prevent them from distracting and being distracted by peers. This contrasted the seating of other students, whose desks were positioned side-by-side.

The use of partitioning was uncommon during movie filming, because groups defined their own workspaces. Students were scattered throughout all spatial zones of the classroom. Only on certain occasions were students isolated from their peers (e.g. Joshua sat outside the classroom door following a power conflict). The low regulation of student movement, and the absence of partitioning reflected the shared distribution of power and control among the students during multimodal designing. The point here is that during movie making, power was constituted differently through new architectonic configurations of the social space.

These architectonic patterns – the material space and its meanings – are important, because they functioned to frame the students' interactions. For example, in the following transcript the boys transform meanings embedded in their static movie sets and characters, to add the dimension of time through a three-dimensional sequence of movements. The boys stood facing the digital camera, which was mounted on a tripod and angled at the first movie set on a desk.

Jack:	[Turns around and faces the camera, looking at camera which has automatically switched itself off with the delay. The other boys also turn around.] Oh God!
Nick:	Oh! [Flaps arms]

[The teacher approaches the boys]

Nick:	[Surveys set]. Everything is ready, Ok. [Hands outstretched, palms facing upward]. Oh! Starfish, the starfish! [Moves quickly towards the set to adjust a fallen starfish. Mark puts one hand on his arm to restrain him, and Nick glances back at the camera to make sure that Jack has not taken a photo of his back] Wait – no – the starfish!
Teacher:	Hang on! Hang on! Stop! [The boys freeze] Just check exactly what you've got to do. Now, you can't wait too long, or the camera will just turn off again, so it's really hard.
Nick and Jack:	Yeah.
Teacher:	Now, ah. When you get to the swimming scene, I want you to make sure this tripod remains exactly in the right place, and that you use that tripod [In front of the swimming set]. Ok. Because if you move this, when you come back to it [To reuse the set in scene 3] it will be different again.
Jack:	Yeah.
Teacher:	Make sense?

Boys: Yeah. Right.
Teacher: Make sure you don't bump these [Lamps], because it
                   will affect your lighting.

Jennifer explicitly directed the boys to monitor certain architectonic
structures necessary for meaning-making during filming. For example,
she cautioned that the tripod and lamps needed to remain exactly in the
same place throughout filming. This was necessary to maintain constant
background scenery and lighting. The boys appropriated the material
environment of the filming studio in ways that reconstituted the social
space in different ways.

For example, the architectonic structures (e.g. lights, filming studio),
technologies (e.g. camera, tripod) and the students' bodily uses of the
physical space (e.g. moving away from the viewfinder during shots) mediated the boys' situated engagement in multimodal designing. This production of the social space differed significantly to the writing lessons. In
these lessons, students worked independently and silently at their desks,
using pencils, while generally being unable to stand or speak without
being nominated by the teacher.

The boys continued to film throughout a two-hour period, gradually
becoming more proficient with the filmic medium. The potentials of the
new technologies and architectonic spaces for multimodal designing were
more fully realised.

Mark: The sunscreen man is too far away. Come in a bit! And that
              dude is really looking tall [in relation to the other characters]
Jack: You reckon? [The boys stand back and survey the movie set]
Nick: [Moves to look through lens] It needs to be zoomed out.
              [Adjusts zoom function on the camera]
Jack: Does it? Mark, can we put his arms like that? [Animates the
              arms of the plasticine man so that they appear to be swinging]
Mark: Ok.
Nick: It's zoomed in now [Moves back from camera].
Mark: Yeah. There, there, there! [Pleased with composition]
Nick: Zoom in a tick. Zoom in a tick [Moves to stand with Mark on
              the sidelines].
Jack: No – just wait. [Adjusts the position of some background
              animations to sustain rhythms of movie] Ok.
Mark: Go! [Nick takes photo]
Mark: Again
Jack: Make sure it's even.

Mark: Now [Nick takes second photo. Two photos of each shot must
               be taken].
Nick: That's two [Walks over to Matthew, who is recording].
Mark: [Brushes his hands together as if congratulating himself and
               the team for a job well done]
Matthew: [Dutifully records on the photo schedule]

Filming involved the conscious manipulation of symbolic material within new socially organised practices established among the group. Mark applied his competency with visual and spatial design to achieve balanced proportions of objects within the screen layout. Nick applied his technical knowledge of the digital camera functions to frame the photo-composition. Jack applied his knowledge of gestural design to create realistic animations, while Matthew maintained a log of the shots taken within each scene. New architectonic spaces, that were initially consciously monitored, became naturalised and taken-for-granted within the social space.

Clearly, new multimodal forms of production required transformations of the material space and organisation of the classroom. For students to be inducted into hybrid and specialised digital practices, changes to the architectonic functions and meanings of the classroom space were essential. The generation of new social spaces opened up the potential for representing a multidimensional world through the collaborative production of the social space.

Screen Spaces

I use the term 'screen spaces' to refer to the socially constructed spaces of screen-based media. Screen spaces became important sites for the representation of meaning during the post-production stage of film making. In this section, I aim to highlight the working of power in the character relations depicted in the final movie – *The Case of the Disappearing Pimples* – as they appeared on the screen.

Sarah and Meliame appropriated screen spaces to depict certain character relations – how the movements of people and objects show interactive or relational meanings. There was a sudden appearance of a new character in scene three, when the movie characters shared healthy food in a living room. During filming, the girls had decided that the plot required the brief appearance of a fifth character as a visitor.

The teacher permitted the girls to borrow Daria's figurine, which was of a similar, even slightly superior, quality of workmanship. Sarah and Meliame constantly animated the four original characters – changing postures, eating and moving in solidarity with one another. Even when

Elizabeth and Emma were absent, Sarah and Meliame animated the characters on behalf of their peers.

Daria's character, however, was defined by the absence of life and movement. Her dark-haired character was relegated to the sofa, where she remained idle, visually and spatially marginalised as 'other'. Several times during the making of the film, I drew attention to this absence of movement:

Researcher: Make sure the one on the couch moves a bit.

[Later]

Researcher: Is the purple one going to get some food?
Sarah: Na – it's not hungry.

Sarah's response explained why Daria's character was not incorporated into the activities of the group on this occasion. Yet it masked the differentiated character relations that were represented on the screen. The marginalising spatial patterns continued throughout the third scene, with the four figures turning their gaze towards one another as members of the clique. In contrast, the fifth character was moved to the table only when the others had finished eating, and were reclining on the sofa.

Curiously, the gaze of Daria's figure was frequently turned away from the other characters and the camera. This was the only character ever photographed from back view – an angle which Kress and van Leeuwen (1996) argue is often used to indicate the strongest degree of detachment from viewers. Consciously or uncritically, wittingly or unwittingly, Sarah and her peers drew upon screen spaces to distance the non-member from the clique.

I cite this to demonstrate the way in which screen spaces are socially constructed sites, where power relations between the identities of the screen do not escape the culturally constructed power configurations of the world (Valk, 2008). All screen spaces are fundamentally mediated by power relations, which are socially and historically constituted. Social relations involving power are entailed in any representation on the screen, including those produced by youth. The girls were implicated in the social reproduction of power and relations of domination and subordination, in which we all participate.

New Social Spaces

This chapter is significant because it forges new understandings about the transformed production of social space through multimodal designing. The multiliteracies classroom created new social spaces, which I have categorised as dialogic, bodily, embodied, architectonic and screen spaces. The production of new social spaces both mediated, and was mediated by, engagement of the actors in digital and multimodal forms of representation. This occurred in a reciprocal way, creating different potentials for learning.

It was demonstrated in this chapter how 'dialogic spaces' of authorship were created when the students incorporated their own stories or internal dialogisations of their ideas and experiences into multi-voiced classroom narratives. This dialogic pedagogy contrasted with the grammar lessons involving direct instruction, in which students became passive recipients of the teacher's monologue.

Specific 'bodily spaces' or displays of orientation – participants' uses of gaze, posture, gesture and other modes – suggested different kinds of engagement with curricular objects and individuals than during periods of direct instruction. Rather than a limited range of postures that are required when students listen to the teacher, multimodal designing allowed individuals to communicate holistic bodily engagement with divergent, yet simultaneous operating displays of orientation. For example, they negotiated movie designs with their peers, while creating movie sets and props with their hands, providing bodily evidence of their productive designing.

The multiliteracies classroom was characterised by transformed 'embodied spaces' through the production of identity artefacts. The students drew upon multiple layers of representational resource, from within their media environment and cultural experiences, projecting new social spaces by reconfiguring their sense of identity through the claymation figures.

Transformations of the architectonic spaces of the classroom – its material qualities of design and structure, such as spatial arrangements of classroom furniture – were required for students to be inducted into hybrid, specialised filmic production. The new architectonic patterns, particularly within the filming studio, constituted a different spatial order, functioning as a resource for the students' engagement in creative multimedia production.

The analysis of screen spaces highlighted the workings of power expressed in the character relations depicted by students. Screen spaces produced by the students were clearly socially constructed sites in which power relations between the created identities of the screen did not escape the culturally constructed power configurations in the students' lives and the wider social system.

Teachers of multiliteracies can dynamically transform the social spaces of the classroom. In the complex transformation of the multiliteracies classroom, digital technologies should not be seen as an end, but as a means for multimodal designing. Multimodal designing was not about experimenting with novel technologies for an unknown future, or for the sake of innovation itself. Students in multiliteracies classrooms are taking up technologies that already dominate the current global communications environment. New forms of multimodal and digital media call for dynamic transformations of the classroom space, itself, a socially produced multimodal text.[1]

Note

1. This chapter is based on the following article: Mills, K.A. (2010a) Filming in progress: New spaces for multimodal designing. *Linguistics and Education* 21, 14–28.

Chapter 6
Discourses and Diversity

Ted grinned at Julia as they filmed their claymation movie and asked, 'Have you seen Lord of the Rings?' The teacher overheard the comment from across the room, and replied, 'Ted, that's got nothing to do with this!' Ted drew upon his indigenous form of language to engage in collaborative literacy practice – one that generated solidarity with others. Nevertheless, what mattered in the institutional context of schooling was who he was, and how he was required to act (Mills, 2006b).

This chapter describes principles observed in the multiliteracies classroom about classroom discourses and its relation to multimodal designing. This dicussion is based on the work of James Gee (1992), which I have applied to the analysis of discourses in the multiliteracies classroom. 'Discourses' is used here to refer to socially accepted ways of displaying membership in particular social groups through words, actions, values, beliefs, gestures and other representations of self. Gee uses a capital 'D' to distinguish this understanding of the term 'Discourses' from its general useage. I use 'discourses' with the same intent, but without the distinguishing capitalisation.

In this sense of the word, discourses are different social languages used in multiple social contexts to present varied social identities. For example, to be a good student, one must think, speak and act like a good student and recognise others who do the same. In such ways, discourses function as 'identity kits' or social roles that one adopts to make oneself recognisable to others (Gee, 1996: 127).

Discourses are vital in the analysis of any new literacy pedagogy because discourses are always tied to status or power relations. The conditions or restrictions on students' primary discourses are central to understanding the distribution of access to the new literacies with digital media. This is because discourses give the material world certain meanings, distribute social goods in a certain way and, if misused, privilege certain symbol systems and ways of knowing over others (Gee, 2003).

Consequently, discourses affect the equality or inequality of students' educational and social futures. Despite the far-reaching implications of discourses in education, they are often the result of non-deliberate, unconscious choices of their users (Cazden, 1988).

In this chapter, I first categorise discourses, using Gee's distinctions between dominant and marginal, and primary and secondary discourses. Applying this taxonomy to the multiliteracies classroom, I discuss the degree to which the students from many cultural backgrounds were able to draw from their existing cultural resources.

Dominant Discourses

Control over certain dominant discourses, such as written and spoken English, can lead to the acquisition of social goods such as money, power or status. They are also ideological because they are linked to a set of social and political relationships between people (For discourses and power see: Apple, 1986; Freire & Macedo, 1987; Giroux, 1988; Luke, 1988). Dominant discourses are norms for participation that identify insiders or outsiders to dominant groups (Gee, 1996). For example, consider Michael, an Anglo-Australian, who presents the class weather report in one of the school's year 2 classrooms.

Michael: [Refers to weather chart] Well, on Monday, it was sunny and hot – really hot! And Tuesday it was the same as Monday. And on Wednesday, it was ... hotter than those two. And on Thursday, it was a bit cold. Ah, it was cold and sunny. And on Friday – well today, it's a bit cold, and sunny – actually, really sunny! And I think all of you should be wearing, um ...

Teacher: A jumper?

Michael: I think actually, for today, um, I think you should be wearing tracksuit pants. You could wear a jumper instead of tracksuit pants. And yesterday, I hope you were all just wearing a jumper. And um, on Wednesday, I hope you were wearing just the normal, T-shirt for school, and normal shorts, or dresses for girls. And for Tuesday, it was also very hot, so you should have ... some shorts um, and a T-shirt – school T-shirt. And on Monday – I think it would be the same as Tuesday. Thank you.

Teacher: That was a very comprehensive weather report, wasn't it? Give Michael a clap, please. Thanks Michael.

Class: [Claps]

Michael is familiar with the dominant classroom discourse of the 'weather report', including the appropriate ways of speaking. At seven years of age, Michael is similarly apprenticed into a dominant school discourse for presentation of self through appropriate dress: he is an 'insider' within the culture of schooling. Making deictic reference to the weather chart, which serves as a visual aid to support his speech, he presents the report in chronological sequence (i.e. Monday, Tuesday, Wednesday, etc.). Michael uses comparatives (e.g. hot, hotter, really hot, and sunny, really sunny) with ease.

In the second paragraph, Michael shifts the setting to focus on intricate and contextualised knowledge of what counts as 'normal' school dress, ('I think all of you should be wearing, um …'). Interestingly, the compulsory wearing of school uniforms is a discourse of Australian schooling, pervasive across both public and private schooling sectors. Michael confidently reproduces, with a degree of transformation, a typical school weather report. He creates a hybrid text that extends this discourse to successfully articulate the school dress code.

With elaborate detail, this seven-year-old includes appropriate gender distinctions in the dress code ('… or normal shorts, or dresses, for girls). In doing so, he makes clear the consensual limits of the 'standard' school dress code, reacquainting his peers, and displaying to the teacher, the authority and legimacy of the school uniform. Dominant discourses always build on the uses of language, gestures, ways of presenting self and values acquired in one's primary discourse. They empower culturally dominant students because there is consistency and minimal conflict with their existing discourses.

Primary and Secondary Discourses

I use Gee's (1992) term 'primary discourses' to denote the language patterns and social practices of one's early socialisation in informal contexts, such as the home. When applied to institutional contexts, such as schools, primary discourses can be perceived as inappropriate or inconsistent, depending on their degree of consistency with the dominant discourses of the school. By way of contrast, secondary discourses are the language patterns to which people are socialised within institutions beyond early home and peer group socialisation (Gee, 1996). These contexts outside the home include work, school, peer groups, clubs and other institutional affiliations.

Becoming aware of one's secondary discourses is vital. These formal discourses have proven to be a problematic medium in many culturally diverse, mainstream classrooms, where children bring their own ways of interacting, speaking, moving and valuing from their homes and communities. Consider how typical secondary discourses were used to socialise students to the appropriate ways of speaking and moving in the computer laboratory. This lesson occurred with Jennifer's year 2 class, which she taught the year prior to having the upper primary class.

Teacher: [Claps rapidly. Students repeat rhythm]. Cody! Chris! I know you're new to this classroom, but we have a rule: clap – you stop, you freeze! Doweh, you're not looking in my direction. Henry, you're not looking in my direction. If you have a question, are you going to call out like Rebecca did a minute ago? No! If you have a question, what should you do? Tristan?

Tristan: Put your hand up.

Teacher: That's a really good answer, Tristan. If I'm really busy working with someone else, should you get out of your chair and follow me around?

Class: No! [Chorus response]

Teacher: Should you then call out?

Class: No [Chorus response]

Teacher: No – that's absolutely right! You're logging in, getting into [Microsoft] Word, and then you're typing up. You need to plan … [interrupted] Excuse me! Sit up! You should still be looking at me! [Raised voice] Second time, Chris! Tim, sit up with your back straight, thank you! Getting into Word, starting your typing. Any partners that are arguing over seats, I'll just ask you to come and sit on the carpet. Off you go.

A significant portion of time is devoted to 'inculcating' appropriate group norms or required ways of 'being' in the computer laboratory, particularly for newcomers like Chris (Cazden, 1988). This includes controlling the bodily movements of students such as Doweh and Chris, who failed to converge towards group practices such as 'freezing' when the teacher clapped. It also includes providing the right answers in the right way, such as Tristan's response, 'Put your hand up', which is rewarded.

Participation in the secondary discourses of this classroom involves a highly complex, cooperative, self-adjusting pattern of interaction among participants. The teacher rewards and sanctions the speech and postures of students to ensure that members do not vary from group norms. The multiple sanctions that apply in this teaching context evidently prove difficult for both students and teacher to attend to. Such implicit cultural expectations for speaking and acting must become explicit and transparent to all those who have a stake in education.

Multiliteracies and Discourses

I argue here that a theory of discourses is central to multiliteracies, because a multiliteracies approach acknowledges the multiple ways of communicating for different cultural and institutional purposes. In schools and in society, people must continually shift between sets of related social practices that are matched to appropriate presentations of self (Fairclough, 2000). Multiliteracies draws attention to the way in which literacy is pluralised, because of the existence of multiple, competing discourses and identities in multicultural societies, such as Australia. Respect for cultural difference is a key argument of multiliteracies.

Yet the secondary discourses and tacit classroom norms constrained certain students from contributing successfully to the movie-making lessons (Mills, 2006b). For example, consider the following questioning sequence about the visual design elements of a Big Book entitled *Lester and Clyde* (Reece, 1976).

Teacher:	What has the illustrator done here to show you that it's not a very nice pond? Ted? [Hand is up]
Ted:	Um, it looks like the rubbish has been chucked in there.
Teacher:	But how did the illustrator show that. How did they do it?
Ted:	Oh, by ah, like, just chucking stuff in there.
Teacher:	What? Did the illustrator throw things in there?
Ted:	No.
Teacher:	Or did they draw pictures?
Ted:	Yeah.
Teacher:	Well, then you need to explain it. Can you say, 'They drew pictures of rubbish?'
Ted:	They drew pictures of rubbish.
Teacher:	Harry?
Harry:	They drew the pond and the leaves and that to make it look rotten.
Teacher:	It looks a little bit rotten, but what tells you … I can even see that it smells. What has the illustrator done to show you that it smells?

Ted drew upon his primary discourse, using the phrase 'chucking stuff' in the context of this whole class instruction. Ted may have been unfamiliar with how picture books are produced, not realising that an illustrator had imagined the story and visually depicted refuse. Following her initial response to Ted, 'What?' she challenged Ted's statement, asking him to revise his answer, and elicited the correct response from him through repetition. Ted repeated the teacher's version of his statement as requested, echoing the teacher's discourse (Gee, 1996). The teacher deferred the original question to Harry, an Anglo-Australian student, who supplied the appropriate answer (Mills, 2006b).

Ted had mastered oral discourses to win solidarity with others, both peers and adults. For example, I met Ted by chance in a local suburban shopping centre during evening trading hours. He had almost finished selling a box of fundraising chocolate bars to idle cashiers at clothing boutiques, because he was successful in the persuasive discourse of 'marketisation' (Fairclough, 2000: 163).

However, Ted differed from expected classroom norms with respect to his Indigenous Australian primary discourse. His speech was characterised by the use of an informal dialect that was evident when using bound morphemes (-ing), such as 'Watcha doin'?' or 'We've been wastin' a whole million watchin' her doin' her shoes'.

The forms 'watchin'' and 'doin'' signal greater solidarity with, and less deference towards, the listener, treating him or her as a peer, friend or equal. Speakers reflexively combine various degrees of 'in' and 'ing' in a stretch of language to achieve the desired level of solidarity and deference (Gee, 1993; Labov, 1972).

This discourse possessed meaning in the social context of Ted's community – a culture that has retained substantive ties with an oral cultural tradition. Nonetheless, it did not belong in the repertoire of dominant discourses considered appropriate in the institutional context of schooling. Ted's oral language could have been regarded as a potential channel to other forms of literacy (Mills, 2007).

Ted unwittingly violated the discursive patterns or rules that governed what could be said or remain unsaid, and who could speak or remain silent at certain times in the classroom. For example, Ted was habitually admonished for 'unsolicited replying' – calling answers without being nominated by the teacher. Interestingly, unsolicited replying is a common Indigenous Australian discourse pattern (Cazden, 1988). This occurred in the context of lessons in which the teacher's monologue was predominant and controlled the topic of discussion (Mills, 2006b).

Ted had not adopted the identity kit of a Western student – the dominant ways of behaving, dressing and becoming a student (Gee, 1996: 127). For example, he often forgot to remove his hat when indoors and was unable to efficiently carry out practical duties to help the teacher. Jennfier coined a nickname 'Travelling-at-will Ted Doyle'. He constantly looked for legitimate ways to subvert the boundaries of the discourses of the classroom, such as getting a drink during the teacher's monologue, borrowing stationery from peers or asking to go to the toilet block during lessons. The important point is that Ted's primary discourse was corrected because it was not consistent with the secondary discourses of the classroom.

Similarly, Paweni was unfamiliar with the secondary discourses of the classroom, having only been in Australia for one year. During storyboard designing Paweni's group was invited by the teacher to share their movie plans.

Teacher:	Sounds to me like you two [Points to Joseph and David] are doing a lot of the thinking. What's Paweni done today?
Joseph:	She's ...
David:	She's just ...
Rose:	She's trying to ...
Teacher:	Ok. Paweni, can you tell me what you're doing today? What's your job?
Paweni:	Mum.
Teacher:	You're going to be the mum? [Character in the movie plot]
Children:	Yeah.
Teacher:	And are any of these your ideas today? Have you got any suggestions? Have you thought about what we should use on the set? Are you going to have trees? Are you going to have hills?
Joseph:	That's what she's thinking.
David:	Yeah!
Teacher:	Can you make sure that Paweni has some suggestions?

The teacher praised Joseph and David for their favourable contributions to the storyboard, which contrasted Paweni's seemingly negligible participation. Paweni's peers advocated on her behalf, making incomplete defences that appealed to Paweni's effort ('She's', 'She's just', 'She's trying to'). In doing so, they identified and empathised with her different life-world, cultural and language experiences (Mills, 2007). The teacher quizzed Paweni with five rapidly spoken, consecutive questions (beginning with 'And are any of these your ideas today?'). These statements required Paweni to give a verbal account of her contribution to the design. During my time in the field, Paweni rarely spoke more than two words in sequence, and these were generally common nouns or verbs (Mills, 2006b).

Paweni needed the linguistic and cultural resources to respond to the teacher's complex questioning, and so remained silent. Joseph offered an account in Paweni's defence ('That's what she's thinking'), and David demonstrated cultural inclusiveness by supporting Joseph's defence ('Yeah'). While Joseph's subjective claim appealed to Paweni's thought processes, its validity was confirmed by her creative contributions to the visual aspects of the design. Paweni possessed sophisticated artistic abilities and had reworked sections of the backdrop to refine the group's visual representations (Mills, 2007).

Paweni's facility with the dominant discourses of Western schooling was put to the test. By default, the gateway was open to confident users of the dominant discourse, but inaccessible to the non-native – one who was not born in the dominant culture. Essentially, there existed a tension between the dominant, secondary discourses of the classroom and Paweni's primary discourses, identity and Thai culture with which she was still closely connected (Mills, 2006b).

Use of the dominant 'IRE' pattern of discourse also influenced the way in which Paweni was assessed in the following whole class interaction (Mehan, 1979). This occurred in the context of the shared reading of the Big Book *Lester and Clyde* (Reece, 1976).

Teacher: Tell me two things about Lester. I'm going to be asking Ted and Paweni this time [Paweni has been silent]. Paweni, tell me two things about Lester?

Paweni: [no response]

Ted: Old [unsolicited response]

Teacher: Definitely not old. Clyde's old. Don't tell her. What are two things you can tell me about Lester the frog? [Long pause]. I'll come back to you. Ted – two things?

Ted: He's smaller and cheeky.

Teacher: He's smaller and he's cheeky, Ok! Paweni, anything else you can tell me about Lester?

Paweni: [No response]

Teacher: Listen to the sentence. 'Lester is smaller, and he's a lot of fun – a naughty, a cheeky, a mischievous one'. What can you tell me about Lester?

Paweni: [No response]

Teacher: Is he a good frog?

Paweni: No.

Teacher: So what tells you that he's not a good frog?

Joshua: Because he's ... [Unsolicited response]

Teacher: I'm asking Paweni, thank you. Who can tell Paweni what words there tell us about Lester? [No response from Paweni] Ted?

Ted: [Mumbles response]

Teacher: I can't hear you? Sit up, Ted.

Ted: He reckons that he has fun.

Teacher: He's full of fun, but I want to know, 'What words there tell that he is not a good frog? Sarah?

Joseph: Mischievous.

Teacher: Mischievous.

Joshua: … and naughty.

Teacher: And naughty – thank you! Did you hear that Paweni – naughty and mischievous? They're the words that we just read, and that's describing him.

Paweni did not make 'successful' contributions to the IRE discourse common in Western schooling. She did not have sufficient linguistic resources in English to comprehend or describe the attributes of the character in the story. Paweni's silence at question time was tied to difference rather than deficit. Her social identity was constituted in her Thai language and culture, which was not required. An IRE discourse pattern, used in the context of a didactic pedagogy, did not apprentice Paweni to the forms of language that could afford her status in the classroom. What was needed was the recruitment of her existing meaning-making resources, and the social identity it signified (Gee, 1996; Mills, 2006b).

Goldenberg's (1992) research suggests that an appropriate discourse for second language learners is 'instructional conversations'. Through talk that resembles dinnertime conversation, students and teachers interact with one another in a joint meaning-making process, initiated by the students. During instructional conversations the students can lead the interactions while the teacher participates as an equal, contrasting the Initiation–Response–Evaluation interaction patterns discussed earlier (Mehan, 1979).

A single theme is addressed, there is activation and building of the students' knowledge or schema of the topic, and the conversation is open-ended (e.g. fewer known answers provided to questions). The teacher promotes and supports more complex language, and the teacher is responsive to students' contributions (Bauer & Manyak, 2008). For example, pairs of students could turn to one another during the reading of the story to talk about their personal experiences of ponds and frogs. Goldenberg and Patthey-Chavez (1995) found that second language learners who participated in instructional conversations talked more in class and were better able to express themselves.

Another helpful strategy that could have been used in the above lesson is literature logs. Students with limited English can be encouraged to write or sketch their ideas in a literature log before participating in discussions, allowing them to rehearse their verbal contributions.

During audio designing, the teacher provided Paweni with the unique opportunity to present a vocal recording for a community audience. The teacher could have chosen native English speakers in the group to take the roles in the voice recording, but gave special access to Paweni to develop her oral language fluency.

Paweni:	'Look out for cars!' [Deepened accent]
David:	'Ok. Mum'. [Infant voice]
Paweni:	'Watch out – run!' [Staccato rhythm]
Teacher:	No! Remember – we're just recording this bit – this snippet. Let's listen to how clear you were, and if there's background sound [Replays]. Could you hear Paweni?
David or Joseph:	Yes.
Teacher:	Clearly? No! You need to speak clearly. I know English is a second language, so this is hard for you. 'Look out for cars' … ['Cars' said with two syllables, high to low intonation]

[Later]

Paweni:	'Watch out – Run!' [Staccato rhythm].
Teacher:	No!
Teacher:	'Watch out – Run!' [Smooth joins]
Paweni:	'Watch out – Run!'[Monotone]
Teacher:	Doesn't sound like you're yelling. Try it again. 'Watch Out – Run!'
Paweni:	'Watch out – Run!' [Drama in voice, but pronunciation unclear].

[Later]

Paweni:	'Watch out – [Pauses to view script] Watch out – Run!'
Teacher:	'You've only got three words to remember!' [Frustrated tone] 'Watch out run'. You don't need to look at it! [The script]

When the teacher asked the boys if they could hear Paweni clearly, Joseph and David moved to support her ('Could you hear Paweni?' 'Yes'). The teacher corrected Paweni's early approximations of the linguistic speech text, but also took into account that English was a second language for her ('I know English is a second language, so this is hard for you'). After multiple unsuccessful and frustrating rehearsals, the teacher implored that Paweni should be able to remember three words without referring to the script ('You've only got three words to remember! You don't need to look at it!').

Understandably, the teacher's patience was tested on account of the intense scaffolding required to focus Paweni on the nuances of audio design. The teacher provided explicit feedback on the duration of the recording ('Remember – we're just recording this bit – this snippet'), volume ('Could you hear Paweni?'), vocal rhythms ('Watch out – Run!'), and expression ('It doesn't sound like you're yelling. Try it again').

Paweni had come to school with a different language and dialect, and this affected the way she performed (Cook-Gumperz, 1986). Learners like Paweni are expected by the educational system to acquire mainstream discourses extremely late in their education. Students such as Paweni require explicit instruction or meta-knowledge to render them consciously aware of what they are being called upon to do (Gee, 1996).

Sociocultural research has highlighted the need for literacy pedagogy to make use of students' existing competencies and familiarity with literacy events as a resource. For example, teachers can activate and build students' background knowledge through the use of visuals, hands-on experiences before the reading of texts, gestures, dramatisation, demonstrations and graphic organisers (Bauer & Manyak, 2008). Students from marginal groups can then be moved systematically towards powerful literate practices that are essential for community life, scholastic achievement and occupational access (Anstey & Bull, 2004).

On several occasions, students of the dominant, Anglo-Australian ethnicity initiated conversations with peers that were inclusive of ethnically marginalised students.

Paweni: That's more big. [Erases the existing drawing of a road on the movie set] Here. Here. [Paweni uses a ruler to measure a wider, straighter road.]

[Later]

David: Paweni – that road's too big.
Joseph: Very … big.
Rose: Way, way, way, way, way, too big!

[Later]

Joseph: Can we just turn it over?
David: No [There is paint on the back].

Joseph: Can we turn it over?
Paweni: Wait – too big! [Paweni rubs out the lines as others watch].

In this example, Paweni initially confused the comparative form of the adjective 'bigger' or 'too big' with 'more big' ('That's more big'.). Her peers accepted Paweni's approximation because they understood Paweni's difficulty with English speech patterns. Yet they proceeded to demonstrate alternative comparative forms – 'too big', 'very big' and 'way too big' – speaking slowly and with repetition to build her repertoire of linguistic resources (Mills, 2007).

The children succeeded in scaffolding Paweni's speech to enable her to gain access to the discourse in an inclusive way, demonstrated by Paweni's learning. At the end of this interaction, she chose a suitable comparative form – 'Wait, too big!' Paweni's fledgling utterances were an invitation to other children to anticipate with her in sense making, to achieve solidarity with her – and they moved to accept this invitation (Mills, 2006b).

In contrast to the previous examples of marginalised discourses in the year 6 classroom, there were many instances in which students of the dominant culture successfully used the secondary discourses of schooling. For example, a support teacher focused the attention of two Anglo-Australians on appropriate vocabulary for their movie script.

Support Teacher: What are you saying?
Sarah: She's going to take the person who has pimples who is [Acted by] Meliame. She's going to take her to the shops to buy all stuff.
Elizabeth: Yeah
Teacher: Ok. And what are, what are you going to say? 'Let's go to the shops'.
Elizabeth: 'Do you want to put something on to, ah, to try this stuff on your face?'
Sarah: And ah …
Support Teacher: 'Do you want to get some of this *stuff* on your face?' Is that a nice job for the preppies? [Preparatory school audience] Prep school children are aged five. Are you going to have them listening to you saying, 'Are you going to come and get this stuff?' No!
Sarah: No, you would say, 'Would you like to come to the shops and buy some of the cosmetics?'
Support Teacher: 'Some cosmetics!' [Pleased tone of voice]

The support teacher expected the girls to design a verbatim script for their movie, and modelled the required discourse ('Let's go to the shops'). The teacher did not accept Elizabeth's colloquial discourse in terms of its suitability for the intended audience ('"Do you want to get some of this *stuff* on your face!" Is that a nice job for the preppies?'). The girls readily switched to the dominant discourse, constructing a stretch of 'standard' English speech ('No, you would say, "Would you like to come to the shops and buy some of the cosmetics?"'). This dominant language satisfied the support teacher ('Some cosmetics!'). A similar pattern was observed in a subsequent conversation between the support teacher and the girls.

Support Teacher:	Good. Ok. And what else is going to be said?
Elizabeth:	And then, 'Do you want to buy some fruit?'
Support Teacher:	'At the, at the' – Oh, I see! [Observes the backdrop of a supermarket]
Emma:	We've also got a party, there's a big party!
Support Teacher:	By gee! You're leaving your work extremely late! Well, you need to really, really, really, I don't know. I don't know how on earth you're going to finish everything!
Sarah:	Miss Taylor said, ah …
Elizabeth:	We've got a lot of time. We've been working really hard!
Support Teacher:	Oh, Ok, Ok – that's fine!

There is a sense in which the support teacher's interaction with the girls reflected parent–child conversations in middle-class, Anglo-Australian homes. These interactive 'fill-in-the-blank' discourses build towards more descriptive and lexically explicit detail (Gee, 1996). The students drew from the repertoire of literacy practices built into their home cultures – practices that resonated with a certain type of schooling. Sarah and Elizabeth were not overtly aware of the IRE pattern in school-based discourses, but they were proficient in engaging in the adult–child scaffolding of interactions. This is because the school similarly valued the cultural capital they had acquired in their home (Mills, 2006b, 2007).

These culturally and linguistically dominant students were able to formulate the required language within the parameters of the secondary discourses of the school. This is because they had experienced a significant history of enculturation into the social practice of schooling and ways of interpreting experiences. This apprenticeship afforded them particular language forms, including familiarity with the routines of schooling.

These forms of language embody meanings owned, shared and inhabited by dominant groups in society (Gee, 1992; Mills, 2006b).

Culturally and linguistically dominant students had the advantage of being able to report on their work to satisfy the expectations of the teacher. They were selected to become spokespersons for groups. They gained control of classroom discussions by raising their hands – 'David, I see your hand up – you're in control'. Such ways of acting and speaking in the classroom are considered *de rigueur* and successful in schools.

Similarly, students gained rewards, status and power when they sat upright with their hands resting atop their heads and assumed other required postures. For instance, the teacher utilised discourses to elicit certain bodily movements and postures required of students as addressees: 'Everybody turn to face him please', 'Wait until everybody is sitting on their bottoms, and actually look like listeners please' and 'Thanks to those people who are sitting up nicely ready to listen'. Through such *modus operandi*, dominant students frequently gained greater access to multiliteracies than those who were less familiar with social and cultural expectations.

Interestingly, culturally dominant students reproduced the secondary discourses of the classroom to control interactions among their peers. For example, Julia used imperative statements to manage her collaborative group, such as, 'You had better move along then'. When called upon to report their progress to the teacher, David satisfied the teacher's expectations with the riposte, 'We're on task'. Speech alone was not singularly important, but an amalgamation of being the proper type of person, from gestures to grooming. Like most institutional contexts of schooling, making sense required appropriate listeners and speakers, or readers and writers, to recruit meaning in ways that were implicitly value-laden (Gee, 1996).

In contrast, Ted, Paweni and their ethnically marginalised peers had not acquired the cultural capital that was valued in the school. They did not have mastery of the school-based social practices, with requisite ways of interacting and valuing, that the school and mainstream culture rewards (Gee, 1992; Mills, 2006b).

They did not have time to gradually 'pick up' these skills and rituals as concomitant to the apprenticeship process, because they had not been socialised into the required ways of being in the classroom that were intimately associated with the social identities of the dominant culture. Insiders of the dominant culture succeeded in this environment because they knew the hidden rules of the game. Outsiders to the dominant power did not. In this complex of social, cultural and power relations, access to a widened repertoire of literacies was unintentionally limited.

New Discourses

This chapter has shown that secondary discourses of the classroom were more accessible to children from Anglo-Australian, middle-class backgrounds, because these discourses were congruent with learners' experiences outside of school.

Despite the teacher's well-informed efforts to enact the multiliteracies pedagogy and provide opportunities for new digital media design, not all learners had equal access to all meanings. Rather, meanings were unintentionally distributed along overlapping lines of ethnicity, socioeconomic status, and students' degree of familiarity with the dominant discourses (Mills, 2008b).

The teacher's translation of the multiliteracies pedagogy to classroom practice was not exempt from being implicated in the historical reproduction of class relations. This was because ethnically marginalised students were still less able to draw from their existing cultural resources than culturally dominant students. Consequently, dominant students, proficient with the discourses of Western schooling, gained greater access to multiliteracies than their marginalised counterparts (Mills, 2006b, 2007).

This raises a critical issue for teachers who desire to enact the multiliteracies pedagogy effectively as its proponents intended, while transforming the inequitable patterns of marginalisation so normalised in the schooling system. What can teachers do to transform patterns of inequity in their classrooms, to bridge the gap between the dominant and marginalised cultures?

The New London Group (1996) theorises that equitable access requires the respect of the diverse cultures and prior experiences of students. This orientation towards inclusive classroom practice is only the beginning. The proximity of cultural and linguistic diversity today necessitates that the language of classrooms must change (Mills, 2006c). When enacting any new pedagogy, the multiple discourses of students should be valued in classrooms that are characterised by a supportive cultural community. Gee (1996: 190–191) argues, '... the exclusion of certain students' discourses from the classroom seriously cheats and damages everyone ... Each of us has a moral obligation to reflect consciously ... when there is reason to believe that a discourse of which we are a member advantages us or our group over other people or other groups'.

Chapter 7
Power and Access

Teacher: There will be consequences for your actions today, Simon Bird. You need to prove that you're working, otherwise – watch out! You won't be filming!

The findings in this chapter focus on classroom power relations and their influence on the students' access to multiliteracies. The multiliteracies classroom is a mirror of the larger societal structures and power relations, while consisting of its own dynamic system of power relations and structures.

There is a body of critical research that analyses the working of power in various aspects of education (see critical research on power: Anderson, 1989; Apple & Weis, 1983; Popkewitz & Guba, 1990; Quantz, 1992). These studies share common sociological roots in critical theory, which begins with the recognition that certain groups in any society or social setting are privileged over others. Critical research aims to uncover the subtleties of oppression so that its invisible nature is revealed, challenged and transformed (Carspecken, 1996).

A key assumption of critical research is that power relations mediate all action (Carspecken, 1996). In other words, all acts demonstrate a person's power to determine one course of action over another, causing a degree of change, either great or small (Giddens, 1979, 1984). For example, the normative power of the teacher – the status of the teacher in the culture of schooling – may be all that is needed to engender compliant behaviour from students. Students obey the teacher because society says that they ought to. However, if a student chooses to consistently resist the teacher, the teacher's normative power becomes ineffectual. The teacher may call upon other forms of power, such as personal charm, to win the loyalty of the student, or coercive power, threatening sanctions (penalty) for certain behaviours (Carspecken, 1996). While all action is tied to power, actions vary by degree of power.

Imagine that the teacher cautions a student, who is found bullying children on the playground, that if they continue this behaviour, they will not be permitted to attend the school camp. Even though this is a situation involving strong coercion, the student retains some power to resist the school rules. Giddens (1984) argues that any analysis of power must account for both the power inherent in social structures, such as schools, as well as the power inherent in the actors, in this case students and teachers, who through their actions can make some difference in the world. In this way, power is inherent in the actions of all participants, rather than the exclusive property of institutions, and can be intentional, unintentional, constraining and enabling.

In light of this, McLaren's (1993) theory of resistance provides theoretical categories which are used here to interpret the actions of certain students. The critical ethnographic research of Willis (1977) and later, McLaren (1993) illustrated the power possessed by individuals to resist the structural power of the school. Willis's (1977) Learning to Labour acknowledged the development of an anti-school culture through the volition of boys who drew upon familiar cultural themes in response to institutional constraints. In this way, the boys were not merely powerless subjects unwittingly dominated by the power of the institution.

McLaren (1993) coined the terms active and passive resistance which are used in this chapter to account for the agency of individuals to resist structural power. For example, students may argue in direct confrontation with the teacher. This constitutes active resistance, since it is an intentional attempt by a subordinate to subvert or sabotage the normative codes of the dominant school order. Conversely, two students may offer to run errands for the teacher because they don't know how to begin their writing task. This is passive resistance, since students unconsciously subvert or sabotage the normative codes. Another example of passive resistance is when abiding by the rules is temporarily overridden by the momentary stimulation of conversation with a peer (Cazden, 1988). McLaren's (1993) theme of resistance emphasises the agency of students, serving to balance any focus on the subordinate position of students within the power structures of the school.

It is demonstrated here how the teacher's use of power had a significant and consistent influence on the students' access to multiliteracies. Comparisons are made between the learning that occurred for students of the dominant, Anglo-Australian, middle-class culture, and for those who were from economically marginalised backgrounds.

Power and Excluded Learners

A series of events and complex power relations lead to the exclusion of five boys from continuing movie making. The implications of these events on the students' access to multimodal designing were significant.

From the outset of the movie-making process, there was continual conflict among the three boys who designed *Breaking the News*. Tim, Simon and Ben were Anglo-Australian boys from low-socioeconomic backgrounds. Tim had significant learning difficulties, including an inability to concentrate on written work. He had a high level of absenteeism during my fieldwork. On many occasions, he would sit at the door of the classroom refusing to continue his work. The teacher was in the process of preparing written documentation about his learning difficulties to assist a paediatrician to make a diagnosis.

Simon was ascertained through standardised tests as intellectually impaired. He had an Intelligence Quotient below seventy and the school qualified for government-funded learning support on his behalf. Simon was unable to contribute meaningfully to the teacher-directed discussions, even when nominated by the teacher to respond. For example, Simon was unable to articulate the author's purpose for writing the picture book *Lester and Clyde* (Reece, 1976).

Teacher:	The author is telling you about the environment. He's telling us about polluting the pond. So why did he write this book? What did he want children to think, Simon?
Simon:	Trash, [pause] put … pollution.
Teacher:	'Trash put pollution'. What do you mean?
Simon:	[Silence]
Teacher:	Ok. Start it again.
Simon:	[Silence].
Teacher:	Harry?

Simon was unable to organise his thoughts in a coherent and linear way. The cognitive demands of planning a verbal response in his mind, and the social demands of expressing his thoughts in formal discussions proved to be complex. Simon generally followed classroom rules and despite his learning difficulties, would raise his hand to respond to the teacher's questioning.

Ben used an informal dialect of English from his home, including colloquialisms, such as catchin', c'mon, 'cept, 'cause and gonna. He frequently resisted the secondary discourses of the school such as the required ways of acting, moving and speaking in the classroom. For example, during a lesson in the computer room, the teacher interpreted Ben's body language through the following statement.

> We've got about six children who are just lounging around. Look at your body language! [Directly to Ben] You've got your hands behind your head and you're leaning back like you're in the Bahamas. You are so far behind in your work. You haven't got time to scratch yourself!

Ben's body language – swinging back on his chair with his hands behind his head – communicated resistance to the discourse of schooling. Students act multimodally in their sensory and holistic engagement of their bodies – there is no separation of body, mind, and will (Jewitt & Kress, 2003). Such resistance was often demonstrated bodily in the posture of the boys (McLaren & Leonard, 1993). For example, Ben would turn away from the teacher as if he had not heard her instructions, even when she was in very close proximity. Ben was observed slouching in his chair and directing his gaze downwards when he was reprimanded. The students' bodies and gestures showed confinement and constriction when conceding defeat in interactions of unequal power with the teacher (Carspecken, 1996). Resistance was evident holistically in the boys' bodies, as they became sites of struggle (Mills, 2007).

On several occasions, power relations between the three boys – Tim, Simon and Ben – intensified into physical violence with one another, accompanied by swearing in the classroom. The teacher responsibly intervened to create spatial and physical boundaries to separate the boys during these times.

Soon after this event, she negotiated a behavioural contract with the whole class. The students were asked to determine behaviours that would be punished by exclusion from movie making. The following interaction is one of the most significant in relation to power and its attendant relationship to the learners' access to digital and multimodal designing (Mills, 2007). Confronted by the boys' incessantly troublesome behaviours, the teacher addressed the class:

> We need to decide what the punishment is going to be for people who are kicked out of claymation. There are people in the classroom who are constantly getting their names on the blackboard. We've got people with three crosses against their names, and we've had groups today that have been swearing at other people, not cooperating – arguing. This group of boys who were working over here got almost nothing done today, and if it wasn't for me intervening, I'm quite sure there would have been a serious fight.

So Simon, and Ben and Tim – your group is this close from being completely shut down and cancelled [shows small gap between fingers], because I'm that unimpressed with the work that you're doing. So what should be the cut-off? Should it be that when you have a certain number of crosses against your name on the blackboard that you don't get to film? Should it be if your movie set is not finished by the end of next week, you don't get to film?

This simple linguistic exchange brings into play a multifaceted and consequential mesh of historical power relations. The power relations exist between the teacher as speaker, culturally endowed with a specific social authority in the school, and the student group as the subordinate audience, who recognise the authority of the teacher to varying degrees (Jenkins, 1992). The point is that these negotiations occurred in the context of unequal power relationships that always exist between the teacher and students within the school institution.

Specifically, the negotiable aspect of this interactively established contract was to determine the number and type of rule violations that would invoke the sanctions, such as arguing on two occasions, or swearing once (Carspecken, 1996). The students were given the power to decide whether individuals or the group would receive the sanctions if one member did not follow the rules. On the other hand, the sanction – exclusion from claymation designing – was clearly not negotiable. The following transcript illustrates the beginning of this negotiation process.

Teacher:	We're going to vote on this as a class. Does anyone else have a suggestion?
Harry:	Yeah, if your name is on the board and you have a cross as well.
Teacher:	So your name and a cross as well, and you should be out. Just that person or the whole group?
David:	Just that person.
Teacher:	Just that person. Anyone else have a suggestion? Because I am sick, I am tired and I'm cranky, and there are people in this classroom I guarantee that won't be filming. 'Cause quite frankly, I don't have time for it'. It's pathetic, the behaviour I'm getting.
Rose:	If you swear you can't film.
Teacher:	So if you're a person who swears, you get kicked out instantly?
Children:	Yeah.

There is a tension evident here between the primary discourse of certain students – those who swear – and the secondary discourse of the school – an institutionally established system of exchange that guides speakers in relation to what can be said within a formal social context. Rose's suggestion ('If you swear you can't film') was accepted because it was consistent with a historically solidified discourse of the school.

During this negotiation process, normalising statements were used to render the sanctions as legitimate for students in year 6:

> For you to be allowed to do claymation, you have to be able to work independently. You don't need to have me there to hold your hand and make sure everyone is feeling nice about themselves and doing the right thing. You're in Year Six!

This operation of normalising discourse – the invoking of a standard of normal or conforming behaviour – rendered the legitimacy of the new sanctions unquestioned (Gore, 1988; Mills, 2007). The outcome was the establishment of three sanctions for violating the rules. The majority of students voted, through a show of hands, that the sanctions would be administered when individuals had three cumulative infringements of school rules within a week. Individuals who swore on one occasion would immediately incur the sanctions. In relation to both sanctions, the students wished only the individual offender, rather than their movie-making group, to be penalised. The teacher also added a third, non-negotiable sanction:

> I tell you right now – the whole group, or any group, who does not have their set, and their props, and their characters finished by next Friday, will not be filming.

The three regulating sanctions prohibited access to digitally mediated designing. The sanctions bounded the students' agency to two actions. They could maintain productivity and follow the rules to gain access to digital movie making. Conversely, they could choose to resist rules and receive the sanctions – namely, to forfeit access to digital media design. These conditions of constraint, while limiting their actions, did not result in the complete dissolution of the students' agency. While power relations appear to bolster the authority of the teacher, the students could still exert counter-power (Mills, 2007).

The following week I returned to the classroom to discover that that several boys had incurred three infringements of school rules, and the teacher had duly enacted the sanctions. A new notice was displayed prominently on a wall of the classroom, differentiating between the students

Table 7.1 Poster naming recipients of sanctions

Groups to film
Slip, Slop, Slap [Nick, Jack, Matthew, Mark],
The Garage [John, Harry, Wooraba],
The Healthy Picnic [Ted, Daria, Julia],
The Case of the Disappearing Pimples [Sarah, Emma, Elizabeth, Meliame],
Crossing the Road [David, Joseph, Paweni, Rose].
Not filming as sets not complete on time: *Breaking the News* [Simon, Benjamin, Tim] (You may display your work completed at book launch but not film).
Not filming because of behaviour: Joshua, Daniel, Simon, Benjamin, Tim

Source: Mills (2008b)

who had received the sanctions and those who had not (Table 7.1) (Mills, 2008b). The poster was a product of the official secondary discourse, which functioned as an institutional form of social classification. It positioned the students within the social hierarchy of the classroom, and constrained them to engage in the routines associated with that positioning (Martin-Jones & Saxena, 1996; Mills, 2007).

This poster served to legitimise and formalise the enactment of the sanctions. It applied exclusion – a technique for tracing the limits that define difference, setting boundaries, or defining zones (Gore, 1988). It named and differentiated the children by three behavioural categories ('Groups to film', 'Not filming – sets not completed on time', 'Not filming because of behaviour').

Pragmatic Horizon Analysis, explained in the Appendix, was applied to the poster. This analytic tool is used here to articulate the objective, normative, and subjective claims in the notice, including the foregrounded (explicit), to backgrounded (implicit) meanings (see Table 7.2).

Simon, Ben and Tim, from the group *Breaking the News*, were listed in both categories of exclusion: for having incomplete sets, and for rule breaking. John, from *The Garage* group, was also excluded for disobeying the sanctions. The teacher would often regulate John's behaviour by punctuating her direct instructions to the whole class with 'John Jackson'. He was a student with high levels of absenteeism during the observed lessons.

Joshua, from the group who created *The Healthy Picnic* was the fifth student to receive the sanctions, described by the teacher as her 'main

Table 7.2 Pragmatic horizon analysis of notice

Possible objective claims
Quite foregrounded, quite immediate
The students in the first list will film their digital movie. The students in the second list will not film because they did not complete their work on time. The students in the third list will not film because they resisted the school rules for behaviour.
Less foregrounded, less immediate
The students will receive different privileges based upon their ability to meet norms (productivity) and sanctioned rules (moral behaviour).
Possible normative–evaluative claims
Less foregrounded, less immediate
Students are required to follow the school rules for productivity and legitimate ways of behaving in the classroom. The teacher has the authority to withdraw the privilege of claymation movie making from the students who do not follow these boundary-maintaining requirements of the system.
Highly backgrounded, remote, taken-for-granted
Students should be differentiated from one another to distribute privileges fairly on the basis of student compliance with expected norms (productivity) and sanctioned rules (moral behaviour). (Also) Filming claymation movies is a privilege that can be withdrawn from students who resist school rules.
Possible subjective claims
Quite foregrounded, quite immediate
I am a fair and reasonable teacher in a position of authority.

behaviour problem'. I constantly observed him seeking attention from both peers and the teacher by moving out of his seat, offering unsolicited replies, and adopting exaggerated gestures and movements that were bodily symbols of resistance to the discourse of schooling. The five boys excluded were from the dominant ethnicity, Anglo-Australians, but were marginal to the dominant culture by reason of their low socioeconomic backgrounds.

The teacher re-emphasised the enactment of the sanctions by making an announcement to the whole class.

The only [whole] group that won't be doing their claymation movie is the 'Breaking the News' group, because they are nowhere near finished their set. So they are now out of the race. They had three sets to make. They made one character and half of one set. So they are not anywhere near being able to catch up. So they will not be able to make their claymation movie. You said that as a group. You voted on it. Joshua and John also have more than two crosses, so they don't get to film as well. So John's group, you still film, but John does not. Ok?

Totalisation – giving a collective character to social practices – was used here to attribute the formulation of the sanctions to the class as a whole ('You said that as a group. You voted on it') (Gore, 1988). The enactment of these sanctions functioned to exclude the economically marginalised boys from the full repertoire of multiliteracies. In the teacher's words, they were 'now out of the race'. The sanctions denied those most resistant to the dominant middle-class discourses of schooling from accessing multiliteracies. More importantly, power operated to sort the students according to their social class location, within the classroom (Mills, 2007).

The full implications of the sanctions became apparent during the following weeks. The remainder of the class continued the digital aspects of movie making, while the five boys finished their story writing or coloured in the drawings. The boys were excluded from six to eight hours of movie set designing, digital filming, audio work and digital editing using moviemaking software.

Monomodal forms of communication, that is, using one mode – words – became a sanction for violating the rules (Cope & Kalantzis, 2000c). This supplanted movie making, which involved multimodal and digitally mediated designing for a genuine audience, developing skills that are valued in the world outside of schools (Mills, 2008b).

The direct consequence of the sanctions was the exclusion of five boys from multimodal literacies that are situated meaningfully within the wider community. These literacies included digital photography, script writing, audio recording, digital editing, and special effects. Instead, the boys were kept occupied with print-based literacy tasks. The exclusion of the boys from completing their apprenticeship in digital movie making, effectively prohibited them from accessing valuable forms of cultural capital. Cultural capital is used here following Bourdieu, of which he states: '… academic qualifications are to cultural capital what money is to economic capital' (Bourdieu, 1977: 187).

Prohibiting access to real-world forms of meaning making for these socioeconomically marginalised boys impeded the transfer of literacy practice to genuine literacy situations in society. The reproduction of existing inequities of class, power and identity was secured through a synergy of institutional structures and individual agency, including the boys themselves.

To prove any long-term effects of this exclusion on the boys' future working lives, a longitudinal study would be required. Yet there was some early evidence of a socialisation process into the boys' visions for their future role in society. The following is a pragmatic horizon analysis of an interview transcript with Joshua, one of the five boys who received the sanctions (see Table 7.3).

Table 7.3 Pragmatic horizon analysis of Joshua's claim

Actors: Joshua and Researcher
This transcript probes Joshua's plans in the future world of work. Joshua has just explained that when he leaves school, he would like to do the same kind of work that his father does.

439	**Researcher:**	Um, what does he [Joshua's Father] do?
440	**Joshua:**	He makes garden hoses … pipes.
441	**Researcher:**	Right.
442	**Joshua:**	You know PPI? [Manufacturer]. Near Geebung. Working for the boss.
443	**Researcher:**	Ok. So is there anything else you might like to do … when you become an adult?
444	**Joshua:**	Work at MacDonald's – Because they earn more.

Possible objective claims
Quite foregrounded, quite immediate
I might work at McDonald's when I become an adult because people who work there earn good money.

Possible normative–evaluative claims
Foregrounded, immediate
People who work at McDonald's should be paid good money.

Possible subjective claims
Quite foregrounded, quite immediate
I would probably work at McDonald's because I will earn money.
Highly backgrounded, remote, taken-for-granted
I am looking forward to leaving school and earning money to buy the things I want.

Joshua, whose father worked as a labourer for a hardware manufacturing company, stated his desire to do the same kind of work as his father. When prompted by the researcher to think of alternatives, he stated that he would like to 'work at McDonald's' when he grows up because he imagines that he will 'get more money'. In this way, the observed social practices in the school were connected to features of the society in general, and the wider system through which society's inequitable conditions and structures are eventually realised (Giddens, 1984; Kaspersen, 2000). The process of social selection is evident here, namely, to legitimate and replicate the dominant factions within the social hierarchy (Grenfell, 2004).

To analyse the workings of power in these classroom events, a valuable tool is Carspecken's typology of power relations. This tool distinguishes between four types of power – normative, coercive, contractual, and charm (Carspecken, 1996). The exclusion of the boys from movie making was mediated by coercive power – the threatening of sanctions by a superordinate to force obedience from a subordinate. The subordinate is expected to comply, not on the basis of the superordinate's status, but in order to avoid an unpleasant sanction (Carspecken, 1996). Carspecken (1996: 131) explains that 'coercion is usually employed within normative frameworks of cultural origin that legitimate it'. For example, the use of coercion is legitimated by the teacher's role as an authority figure within the normative institution of schooling (Carspecken, 1996).

It is important to consider that the use of coercive power alone did not deny students access to multiliteracies, because the learners possessed degrees of agency and could act of their own volition to avoid the threatened sanctions. Parallels can be drawn between these classroom events and Willis' (1977) classic ethnographic research. A culture of resistance was evident among the working class lads in and outside the classroom, precipitated and perpetuated by unequal relations between teachers and students (Mills, 2007).

Similarly, McLaren's (1993) theory of resistance explains how students' episodes of resistance to power worked in juxtaposition with school sanctions to implicate the boys further in their own domination. The use of coercive power was not a powerful or effective strategy to render students either productive or compliant learners. Rather, a loss of access to certain forms of meaning-making was secured, coupled with unintended outcomes, such as increased absenteeism.

The school's potential to empower these economically marginalised students to rise above oppressive forms of work in society was weakened by the boys' acts of resistance' to domination. Relations of power in the classroom were systematically asymmetrical, tied to interactions between coercive power and the boys' acts of resistance to the dominant discourse. This domination was inadvertently masked by inviting the subordinates to negotiate the minor details of the sanctions through an interactively established contract, concealing the teacher's authorisation of the sanctions that prohibited access to multiple modes, media and technologies for communication (Mills, 2007).

Power and Print-based Literacies

It is significant that the use of coercive power differentiated the curriculum for students who violated the school rules, namely, that print-based literacy practices, such as writing with conventional tools, replaced multimodal, digital designing. The teacher's perceptions of monomodal and multimodal literacies are contrasted in the following pragmatic horizon analysis of her dialogue (see Table 7.4).

Here, the foregrounded and backgrounded meanings of the teacher's claims underscore the view that claymation movie making does not constitute normal literacy practice, but instead, is a special privilege or novelty. The teacher understood that digital filming – an activity favoured by the students – was not at the core of the state literacy curriculum. Therefore, it could be legitimately withdrawn to maintain social order in the classroom.

However, all literate practices are not of equivalent power in terms of the socioeconomic gains and cultural knowledge they generate, some having negligible relevance to community and occupational contexts. For example, being able to complete fill-in-the-blank writing exercises is potentially less powerful than specialist proficiencies in multimodal, digitally media design (Bull & Anstey, 2003a).

An important caveat must be made here about the teacher. The intention of this study has not been to critique the teacher, the students, or any other research participants. Rather, in any critical ethnographic research in an institutional setting, the researcher must take into account power relations, and indeed, problematise the workings of power. The teacher was selected for this study because she is an exceptional teacher in her uptake of new pedagogies, media and technologies for multimodal designing.

She sought to implement innovative practices that would 'empower' and liberate her very difficult and diverse class. When analysing these events, I am mindful that power operates in and through all social actors in multiple and contradictory ways, though at times we attempt to disrupt it. Furthermore, teachers frequently act according to an accepted repertoire of social practices that are historically reified in the institution of schooling.

Table 7.4 Pragmatic horizon analysis of teacher's claim

Actors: Teacher to researcher
The teacher talks to the researcher after a movie-making lesson in which some students were not working cooperatively.
Teacher: And I've told my kids that if they get their name on the back wall, **they're not allowed to do claymation. They'll just sit down and do normal work.** Because some of the boys – their behaviour is starting to get out of control.
Those who later received this sanction were given monomodal literacies, such as writing in their exercise books with a pencil and paper, while the others continued with the digital aspects of the claymation movie designing.
Possible objective claims   *Quite foregrounded, quite immediate*   I've told the students that if they break the classroom rules (i.e. name on the back wall) they will not be permitted to continue claymation movie making. Instead, they will do normal work like students in other classes.   *Highly backgrounded, remote, taken-for-granted*   Multimodal designing (i.e. claymation movie making) does not constitute normal work, while writing with a pencil is usual in schools.
Possible normative–evaluative claims   *Foregrounded, immediate*   These students have failed to comply with the rules, so they should receive sanctions – withdrawal of privileges.   *Highly backgrounded, remote, taken-for-granted*   Access to digital multiliteracies can be withdrawn from students who cannot follow the classroom rules because it is a privilege. Print-based literacies are an appropriate sanction for rule breaking because they are mandatory.
Possible subjective claims   *Quite foregrounded, quite immediate*   I am tired of students resisting the classroom rules. They don't deserve to do special activities that I provide like digital filming. I'll give them mundane schoolwork instead.

With these thoughts in mind, it is helpful to contextualise the classroom events within the established disciplinary practices and uses of coercive power throughout the school. The practice of assigning print-based literacy tasks as a sanction for rule breaking was prevalent throughout the school.

For example, the principal had established a whole school behaviour management system in which the students received rewards for avoiding the accumulation of red cards. The red cards were used as a form of coercive power to deter students from transgressing school rules. All students began the year as 'level ones' and could progress to the next level at the end of each quarter or term. The aim was to reach Level 5 by the end of the year. The receipt of one red card impeded a student from progressing to the next level until the following quarter.

At the end of each term, students in the school cohort were labelled and sorted into rooms. Mirroring the events in the observed classroom, these sanctions operated as a disciplinary technique of classification that differentiated groups of students from one another (Gore, 1988).

Students in Levels 2 to 5 received rewards, such as watching a popular children's movie, while level ones completed monomodal literacy exercises in workbooks, such as repeatedly adding suffixes to lists of root words. Again, print-based literacies that were decontextualised from uses of literacy in the real-world were exploited as a form of social control in the school institution, tied to the use of coercive power.

During the pilot study, three students of Maori, Indigenous and African ethnicity, and two economically marginalised, Anglo-Australian students received the Level 1 sanctions, and were labelled by an infant school teacher as the 'naughties' (see Table A.1 in the appendix for a Pragmatic Horizon Analysis of this speech act). The sanctions denied students of marginalised ethnicities – those who had the greatest distance to traverse between their discourses and the discourses of the school, and whose interests are most at stake in education – access to multiliteracies.

Again, power operated as dissimilation by sorting students according to their social class location within the school (see McLaren, 1994). The practice of ability grouping within the school was found to be a constraining form of differentiation, distributing different pedagogies to students in a marginalising way. The low-ability literacy groups received transmissive forms of pedagogy in the form of grammar lessons.

Transmissive pedagogy, while successfully regulating student behaviour, does not foster decision-making, communication, or creative and technological skills that are required to transcend working-class jobs. The low-ability groups were comprised of the culturally, linguistically and socioeconomically marginalised students. This unintentionally contributed to a non-reflexive causal loop that sustained the unequal distribution of multiliteracies (Mills, 2005b, 2007).

This hierarchical system of labelling, sorting and exclusion distributed rewards to students of the dominant, white, middle-class culture, while administering sanctions to those who were outsiders to the culture of power. This historically formalised system of domination, while seemingly legitimate, unintentionally reproduced or solidified patterns of unequal power and disenfranchisement within the wider society. Consequently, the school produced differing kinds and levels of literacy, permitting some students to access multiliteracies while preventing others.

Multiliteracies and Power

The enactment of coercive power prohibited the five boys from being socialised into multimodal, digitally mediated social practices that are valued in contemporary society. A complex network of social, institutional and cultural interactions worked synergistically with the boys' agency to determine the literacies that did or did not became part of these boys' lives. The students' existing cultural knowledge and social power played a significant role in who gained access to multiliteracies and who did not.

Despite the well-meaning intentions of the teacher, and the enactment of new pedagogies, media and technologies, not all learners had access to all meanings. Rather, meanings continued to be distributed and made accessible along the overlapping social characteristics of gender, ethnicity and socioeconomic status, seen within the context of the dominant institutional structure of the school and the society. This confirmed a key principle of critical sociology: Access to knowledge and cultural capital is discursively situated in relations of power (Carspecken, 1996).

The ideal of the New London Group (2000: 18) is to 'provide access without children having to leave behind or erase their different subjectivities'. This chapter has demonstrated how this goal can be coopted by the enactment of coercive power in the school. Coercive power implicitly maintained learners' existing levels of access to multiliteracies as a marginalising practice of social regulation. This was so habitual or natural in the school setting that the principal and teacher established and maintained these marginalising practices as normal, unproblematic and usual. Yet who was included or excluded by the enactment of coercive power was not arbitrary or random; rather, it was tied to the power and status of the learners in the context of the dominant culture.

What does this mean for educators who are confronted daily by students who resist the classroom rules and disrupt the learning of other students? Social power can take many forms, and not all power relations are coercive or heavy-handed. For example, teachers can confidently draw upon normative power, charm or personality, which is built upon relationships of trust with students, or contractual forms of power (Carspecken, 1996).

The point here is not that all power is marginalising. The possibility for providing equitable access to multiliteracies is heightened when educators draw upon noncoercive forms of power (Mills, 2008b). Sanctions are counterproductive when they prohibit learners from meaningful participation in the multimodal and digital textual practices that have real worth in the new times. Taking into account fundamental issues of power can help to explain why students are not equally engaged in learning tasks, despite the equal allocation of resources and opportunities for multimodal designing. It also helps to see how patterns of exclusion in classrooms are tied to relations of power within the society.

The reflexive use of pedagogies in the context of noncoercive power relations can allow for the 'variability of different forms of meaning making' that the multiliteracies pedagogy was intended to serve (New London Group, 2000: 36). In so doing, educators can work towards the productive and creative agency of all students for today and the future (New London Group, 2000).

Chapter 8
New Times

Readers of a single internet news page today can be bombarded with no less than 350 hyperlinks and an accompanying array of thumbnail images. These links are connected to a plethora of news bites and advertisements that simultaneously vie for the reader's attention. The largest images at the top-left of the page are intentionally more visually prominent, with moving images distracting readers from the top stories.

Serving as a metaphor of recent trends in literacy, the internet news homepage elevates multimodality over monomodality. It is dynamic rather than static, non-linear rather than linear, and portable rather than fixed. It is digital, not paperbound, temporary, not permanent, and accessed electronically rather than materially. It is interactive – for example, users can blog their comments, or publish their profile on the web, adopting the role of reader and author. The information is networked rather than unconnected, optional rather than essential, and hybrid rather than conventional. These text features will continue to become more pervasive in the new times.

As print-based practices become increasingly digitalised, the need to justify the teaching of multiliteracies becomes unnecessary. Digital textual practices now dominate commercial, recreational, and workplace contexts. Education is the last place in society to digitalise literacy practices, with the youngest members in educational sites having the least access to the latest technologies for communication. The multiliteracies argument has awakened educators to recognise the inadequacy of literacy programs that focus exclusively on print-based texts, while an expanding array of communications channels characterises the world outside of schools.

Educators like Jennifer know that books and pencils are necessary, but not sufficient, for students to communicate competently in the 21st century. The following is an excerpt from two semi-structured interviews with Jennifer, included here to enable readers to gain an insight into her perspective of multiliteracies.

KM: What is your conception of multiliteracies?
Jennifer: I believe that multiliteracies is using more than just books as a text.
KM: Yes.
Jennifer: So using real life texts. For example, video, DVDs, magazines, newspapers, ah, instructions, cereal boxes – whatever you can get your hands on that has writing.
KM: Ok.
Jennifer: And it's not just words as text, it's also visual literacies. Ah, as in looking at icons – pictorial things.
KM: So different modes?
Jennifer: Yes, or angle shots, camera shots, movies. All of that … to me is multiliteracies. So it's not just sitting down doing guided reading with books – which certainly has a place.
KM: Yes.
Jennifer: I still do that – directional teaching. But it's extending it to more [pause] texts.

Globally, literacy educators are realising that there are fundamental differences between conventional pencil and paper-based reading and authoring, and multimodal designing, which requires the combining of, and switching between, various modes to make meaning in more holistic ways.

As texts change, so must literacy learning. Children, adolescents and adults engage in a much richer repertoire of linguistic practices, modes and media. For example, preschoolers are being taught to read at home through engagement in virtual worlds, where they create their own avatars, decorate and furnish their houses with virtual toys, and read interactive books in these online environments.

In a digital communications environment, narrow conceptions of literacy are vastly inadequate to describe new literacy practices in homes, schools, workplaces, and society today. Previous conceptions of literacy as monolingual, monocultural and monomodal – one language, culture and mode – have been transformed for the new times as multiliteracies (New London Group, 1996, 2000). The cultural dimension of multiliteracies is just as crucial as the new texts, modes and media.

KM: And how about taking into account cultural differences in multiliteracies?
Jennifer: I think it's just about ingrained in everything. I think the flavour of it goes right through the curriculum. Because there are core values, which are basically underlined in what we're teaching.

KM: Yes.

Jennifer: The key values are 'democratic process' – not as in, teaching about the government, but in the sense of working as a team – making decisions democratically.

KM: Mm.

Jennifer: Then there is 'social justice' – which is highly involved with [pause], diversity and cultural diversity, and ah, the same with 'peace'. Being able to cooperate with people regardless of their colour, skin, sex, gender – you know.

KM: Mm, mm.

Jennifer: All of those things – ah, religion. It doesn't matter what grade you're in – these outcomes are ingrained in everything. But you don't do a 'Let's-sit-down-and-learn-about-a-different-culture-now'. I don't think it would work that way.

KM: Yes

Jennifer: When I look for texts and pieces of writing that the children are doing, I've always got culture in the back of my mind – and gender as well.

In a globalised age, access to multiliteracies requires both teacher and students to cross cultural boundaries (New London Group, 2000). Students must be seen as individuals who have at their disposal a complex range of representational resources, grounded in their cultural experiences and layers of their identities. They also need to be able to draw upon different combinations of modes, media and conventions, so that designing becomes more than reproduction.

In Jennifer's classroom, students could avail themselves of complex representation resources, never exclusively of one mode, but of many modes. Movie making involved the students in drawing on prior experiences with the world, with texts, and with others. It involved reconstructing meaning in significant ways for their intended school community audience. The agency of the student groups, their voice, interests, and purposes were central to designing (New London Group, 2000).

KM: Do you like designing things that have words, pictures, movements, or sound at school?

Darles: Yes – because it is fun.

KM: Ok. What are some of the things that you've made?

Darles: PowerPoint, ah, electronic books.

KM: What do they involve?

Darles: Ah, inserting hyperlinks.

KM: Ok. So you know how to make hyperlinks in documents?

Instead of focusing exclusively on stability and regularity in textual practice, sign making becomes a dynamic and hybrid process that allows for creative production (Mills, 2006b). Similarly, students need to be able to utilise diverse modes and media for various social, community and cultural purposes, including those that cross national boundaries (New London Group, 2000).

KM: Do you think girls and boys from different cultures, or children with more than one language, read in the same way as children with one language?

Daria: No.

KM: What do you think might be the difference?

Daria: Well, they've got more languages to remember.

KM: Ok. Would you come into that category, do you think?

Daria: Yeah.

KM: 'Cause you can speak two languages?

Daria: I can speak four.

KM: You can speak four!

Daria: Chinese, English, Arabic, and another type of Arabic [local vernacular]. Like, it's called Otto-tana.

KM: Can you give me an example? How do you say 'Hello?'

Daria: Ah, in Arabic, you say *salama leko*.

KM: Salama leko?

Daria: And in Otto-tana, you say ah, *def*.

KM: That's short and easy. I think I'll go there! [Laughter]

Daria: [Laughter]

Multiliteracies are not about a narrow, univocal, authoritarian grammar that applies to all social contexts. Rather, it accommodates variations in language use across different cultures, and across social groups – occupations, online communities, recreational groups, religious and political affiliations (New London Group, 2000).

KM: Have you noticed any diversity in the way the students access culturally and linguistically diverse texts, such as books, music, dances, art forms in your class?

Jennifer: Ah, the children that I have from different cultures? There are huge differences! Ah, we've just done a cultural diversity unit now.

KM: Yes.

Jennifer: Ah, I found huge differences with the kids with how they approach things, and how they actually viewed what we're doing in class.

KM: Mm.

Jennifer: So one of the children, who has been in the country for a short time, was sometimes embarrassed to have it pointed out that she was different – because she's come from another culture.

KM: Mm.

Jennifer: And other times, was really proud that we were actually discussing in class how we can help and include her.

KM: Mm.

Jennifer: And my students produced a talk on how they show that they value the students from other cultures in our school.

KM: Ok.

Jennifer: Like Onesa in the next classroom, has only been in the country for three months. And he's come from a refugee camp from Egypt for three years, and then he came from the Sudan before that.

KM: Ok.

Jennifer: So the children borrowed my digital camera at lunchtime, and went out into the playground and interviewed children from cultures other than their own. And asked them how they settled into our local area. It's been a huge eye-opener!

Jennifer addressed cultural diversity in the curriculum, with a view to honouring cultural difference.

Despite the teacher's discursive knowledge of the need for cultural inclusiveness, in practice it still transpired that culturally marginalised students were least able to draw from their existing resources. The secondary discourses of the classroom were more accessible to children from the dominant, Anglo-Australian culture, because they were congruent with their experiences (Mills, 2008b). The Sudanese, Indigenous, Tongan, Maori and Thai students were least familiar with the tacit norms and rules for collaborative group work, and those that governed the use of digital technologies. These students took up opportunities for multimodal design when peers or the teacher communicated expectations to them clearly, personally and directly.

The students' access to multiliteracies was influenced by the enactment of new pedagogies, modes, media, spaces, power and discourses in the classroom. While multimodal and multimedia designing opened up new semiotic possibilities, students exercised differing degrees of agency in utilising these opportunities.

A 'dialectic of access' occurred in which there was reciprocal interaction between the agency of the student, and their ability to take up the socially produced learning structures, including the rules and resources for representation. What was needed was a critical reassessment of selective traditions that were implicit in this process, reflexively transforming them in the interests of marginalised groups (Mills, 2006b, 2008b).

Multiliteracies Pedagogy: Making Sense

KM: How do you find the multiliteracies pedagogy framework? Do you use that model frequently? Do you like it? Do you integrate it with other models, or ...?

Jennifer: It's the only one I plan now, because it makes such sense. And ah, yeah I really like it. I've been teaching like that for years, but it just formalised it, and makes it a bit more structured.

This book has highlighted an important distinction to be made between overt instruction and transmissive pedagogy. Overt instruction does not imply direct transmission, drills and rote learning. Rather, it provides learners with explicit information during '... times when it can most usefully organise and guide practice...' (New London Group, 2000: 33). Transmissive pedagogy restricts literacy to formalised, monolingual, monocultural and rule-governed forms of language, impeding the transfer of literacy practice to genuine literacy practices used in society. Additionally, transmissive pedagogy aims for simple reproduction, rather than new meanings through which designers remake themselves. In contrast, the aim of multiliteracies is designing that is never a reproduction of one available design, but a transformation of existing designing (New London Group, 1996).

During the enactment of situated practice, it is imperative that designing is sufficiently scaffolded by expert peers or adults. Teachers need to avoid the misconception that situated practice exclusively consists of implicit teaching methods. Students should not be expected to drift in the direction of a standard form of the language through immersion in practices of communicative significance (Cope & Kalantzis, 2000c).

Jennifer: But as far as, if they have English as a Second Language, they find it very difficult to read the texts.

KM: Mm.

Jennifer: And they need a lot of support with their work in class. So if I'm producing texts and books and posters to use, a lot of them can't decode it.

KM: Yes.

Jennifer: So I have to watch how I'm teaching.

KM: They need decoding help.

Jennifer: Because I have so many learning support children in here, I have to structure everything anyway, so everything is scaffolded.

Timely instruction is needed during situated practice, with higher levels of scaffolding to support ethnically marginalised learners. Situated practice allows for the inclusion of the experiences of ethnically and socioeconomically marginalised lifeworlds. This is because an aim of situated practice is to provide implicit and explicit knowledge of how written language works in many different cultural contexts (Kalantzis & Cope, 2000a). Daria from Sudan discussed her difficulty when communicating cross-culturally.

KM: Have you noticed any difference in the way children from different cultures, or boys and girls read or write?
Daria: Yeah.
KM: What do you think might be the differences?
Daria: Well, people who speak English, they normally ah, they normally like, make sense when they're writing.
KM: Mm.
Daria: ... or reading. But sometimes when you're from a different country, you sometimes don't make sense when you're writing ... You don't make sense to other people. Like, you leave some words out.

The successful enactment of critical framing enables students to interpret the social and cultural contexts of particular designs (Kalantzis & Cope, 2000a). An outcome of critical framing is the ability to analyse the general function or purpose of a text, making causal connections between its design elements – analysing functionally (Kalantzis & Cope, 2005).

KM: Is there a place for critical framing skills, like, say looking at websites and knowing whether something is valid information or not, or even ...?
Jennifer: I think it should be done constantly, it doesn't matter what genre you're teaching.
KM: So you teach children in grade two to be critical about what they read, and you evaluate literature?
Jennifer: Yes, absolutely!
KM: Mm.
Jennifer: Absolutely – pull things apart. When you're modelling new texts, we're also pulling things apart. It doesn't matter what grade you're in – you should be critically analysing things.
KM: Mm, mm. Ok.

Jennifer: We're doing Christmas catalogues at the moment.
KM: So you're looking at the cultural stereotypes in the suggested gift choices and things?
Jennifer: Yes, yes. Mother's Day was also interesting. We looked at photos of mothers in the media, and what they perceived to be mothers, and they critically compared them to their own mothers ...
KM: Mm, mm.
Jennifer: Which you can do at any age.

Jennifer recognised the importance of helping students to analyse the explicit and implicit motives, agendas and actions behind a text or piece of knowledge, which Kalantzis and Cope refer to as 'analysing critically' (Kalantzis & Cope, 2005: 114). Critical framing also involves assisting students to articulate how their cultural position is related to texts and textual practices, analysing the way in which textual practices differ from the values and persepctives of one's own community.

Jennifer: Ah, because of the children that I've got [in my class] particularly. I have to make sure that it's not biased towards certain cultures.
KM: Yes.
Jennifer: And it could be biased by who's missing in the story, and who's not being represented in whatever the piece of writing or visual text is that we're looking at.
KM: Yes.
Jennifer: So it's just a simple matter of using your critical questions and, and pointing it out, and getting the children to think about it when you're using that text.
KM: Mm.
Jennifer: So I don't necessarily discard a text because it's missing cultures, and not, and not catering for cultures.
KM: Yes.
Jennifer: But it's a matter of, Ok. If we ah, looked at this book, or looked at this movie, and it was in a different language, or had a different cultural slant: How do you think it would be different? It's in the questioning.
Researcher: Mm, mm. It's how you use the text and draw out the fact that it may not mention their cultural perspective.
Jennifer: Yes – how you use the text.

With this understanding, ethnically marginalised students can position themselves in relation to 'those who construct and what they construct', seeing themselves independently of any misrepresentations or omissions of their cultural position (Nakata, 2000: 119). Critical framing is a particular challenge for students who must 'code-switch' between several languages (Nakata, 2000: 119).

KM: Do you ever go … to any other language, like your first and second languages? Do you use your first language [*Nu weh*] at home …?

Meliame: No, because none of them know [it].

KM: Oh don't they? [Surprised] How come only you know it?

Meliame: Because I live with my Nanna.

KM: Oh, so your Nanna speaks …?

Meliame: My second language [Tongan]. I speak to my parents in my first language … *Nu weh*.

KM: And do you use English as well in all of those other environments?

Meliame: Yeah, sometimes. Sometimes in English, and usually in Tongan.

KM: Ah, do you find it hard to switch from one to the other?

Meliame: Kind of.

KM: So you change to match … each person you speak with?

Meliame: Yeah.

KM: Ok. Like if you talk to me in Tongan, I won't understand it.

Meliame: Malo e lelei

KM: Did you say, 'Hi! How are you?' or something? [Laughing]

Meliame: I said, 'Hello'

Meliame had learned to code-switch between three languages to negotiate with others across international boundaries. For students like Meliame, critical framing involves viewing texts in relation to cultural messages that differ more significantly across than within cultural contexts.

The strength of the effective enactment of critical framing in Jennifer's classroom was the linking of critical framing to the other three components of pedagogy – overt instruction, situated practice and transformed practice. For example, students were able to stand back from the design process to analyse their own digital movies both functionally and critically for their intended school community audience.

The digital movies produced by the students in Jennifer's class demonstrate that transformed practice is more than the basic reproduction of print conventions, though applying written forms appropriately is still important. Transformed practice differs to good reproduction of knowledge or skills, because it involves transfering meanings to work in other real-world contexts – applying creatively. It involves 'making connections' across experiences, texts, media, modes and cultures, leading to varying degrees of change (Kalantzis & Cope, 2000a).

New Media: New Metalanguages

The findings in this research reinforce the New London Group's argument that narrow conceptions of literacy need to be vastly expanded, along with an extensive vocabulary to describe new digital media forms adequately. Text forms that are increasingly capturing the attention of young and old in recent years include blogging, creating digital animations, podcasting, writing fan fiction, producing manga comics, photo sharing on the net, wordless picture books for adults, communicating with Voice-Over-Internet-Protocol and webcams, and video gaming and game making.

New metalanguages – languages to describe texts – are needed to articulate the salient characteristics of emergent genres, including increasingly more prevalent 'kineikonic' or moving image texts (Burn & Parker, 2003: 56–72). Static texts are increasingly replaced by moving images as the capabilities of everyday digital technologies are expanded, requiring different ways of interpreting and creating knowledge for intended audiences (Mills, 2008a).

Cope and Kalantzis (1997, 2000b) of the New London Group have called for the continued generation of multimodal metalanguages, a call to which scholars and researchers have responded (see Burn & Parker, 2003; Callow, 2006; Hamston, 2006; Hull & Nelson, 2005; Jewitt, 2006; Kress *et al.*, 2001; Stein, 2007; Unsworth, 2006; Watson & Johnson, 2004). These theorists have applied categories of systemic functional linguistics – representational or ideational, interactive or interpersonal, and compositional or textual meanings – to the meta-functional organisation of multimodal texts (Mills, 2009).

A substantial area of literacy research in the future will centre on the continued analysis and description of innovative text forms. While networked social practices and online communities constantly generate new text forms, there will always be certain conventions that draw from what has gone before. The ongoing generation of flexible metalanguages will enable teachers and students to draw both old and new elements consciously into the design process as competent communicators in the new times (New London Group, 2000).

Discourses for the New Times

There is a need to evaluate the inclusiveness of dominant, secondary discourses when enacting the multiliteracies pedagogy. The proximity of cultural and linguistic diversity today necessitates that the language of classrooms must change (New London Group, 1996). This requires a realisation that the lifeworlds of students are inherently diverse and multilayered.

Jennifer: And that was the other thing – our definition of what makes an Australian: Is it that you're born in this country ... or you're a citizen, or if you feel Australian? Because some of the children here are now citizens, but they don't still feel Australian. They still have a huge passion for their first culture.

KM: Mm ...

Jennifer: And we were saying, well, 'Is that wrong or is that Ok?' And the kids were going 'No, that's Ok'. So it was really ... we got some excellent discussion.

KM: So you actually do talk about those issues?

Jennifer: All the time – all the time!

Students possess, not one lifeworld, but a multiplicity of 'overlapping lifeworlds', with distinctive and sometimes contradictory allegiances (Cope & Kalantzis, 2000a: 207). For students of the dominant culture, their induction into specialist domains has been built via rich bridges to their lifeworlds in attenuated forms, such as bedtime stories as a bridge to classroom interactions. These bridges must be constructed in schools for minority groups, who have mastered the codes and conventions of their own communities' literacy practices (Mills, 2006b; New London Group, 1996).

The effective implementation of the multiliteracies pedagogy requires that teachers reflect on and critique the discourses of their own culture. The use of discourses in routine social interactions is typically automatic, intuitive and uncritical. Discourses defend those who use them by speech and behaviour that presents normalcy. When educators act within their discourses uncritically, they draw upon values that unwittingly advantage certain students, while marginalising others (Mills, 2006b).

Teachers who seek to enact the multiliteracies pedagogy successfully have an obligation to gain meta-knowledge about discourses in order to resist unreflexive, routine practices that limit the potentials of students (Mills, 2006b). As Gee (1996) argues, students also need space to juxtapose diverse discourses and to understand them at a meta-level through a language of reflection. Through such an approach to multiliteracies, students can transform and vary their discourses, create new ones, and experience 'better and more socially just ways of being in the world' (Gee, 1996: 190).

Multiliteracies Classroom and Society

A year after leaving the field, I met with Jennifer to discover what had become of the Anglo-Australian boys who had been excluded from movie making during the research. She described how the five boys had engaged productively in subsequent multiliteracies units of work, having realised the negative consequences of their actions during the claymation movie making projects. Jennifer had identified that multiliteracies is vital to engage boys in literacy learning.

KM:	Do you think that multiliteracies poses threats to any other aspect of the curriculum that could become, sort of ah, pushed aside with the new focus?
Jennifer:	Ah, that's a good question. Ah, no – I don't think so. I think that's the only way we can go, especially with our boys in education, you know. I think our boys are suffering, and struggling and technology switches them on.
KM:	Makes it so much more interesting.
Jennifer:	And it's their real life. They play computer games, and they watch and play, you know, DVDs, and watch TV.
KM:	Mm, mm.
Jennifer:	And they're immersed in it. So to come to school and to do nothing but read a traditional book is going backwards, and it's not turning them on ... You need a mix of things. You need, you still need traditional texts. But you need to still move forward.

The exclusion of the boys from the digital aspects of movie making during my time in Jennifer's classroom was apparently short-lived. Jennifer's report of the boys' subsequent engagement in multimedia authorship was a positive one. She also expressed that her understanding and implementation of the multiliteracies pedagogy had continued to develop after I had left the classroom. Yet the use of coercive power was an established disciplinary practice of the school, militating against the provision of access to multiliteracies for all.

Students' access to multiliteracies is theorised here in light of the duality between the actions of the teacher and students, and the enabling and constraining structures in the social system are evident. Access to multiliteracies among the culturally and linguistically diverse class was differential. Their experiences varied on a continuum from reproduction of existing degrees of access, to transformed designing. Pedagogies, modes, media, social spaces, discourses and power in the classroom mediated these experiences, which were in turn influenced by the agency of individuals. The teacher and students were similarly constrained by the meaning structures (e.g. national language), norms (e.g. routine social behaviours) and power relations (e.g. gender, race, class) in the school and wider social system.

The events observed in the multiliteracies classroom confirm a perspective of critical sociology, which is that despite the intentions and efforts of educators, schools are often institutional sites of the reproduction of stratified social inequality (Apple, 1995; Bourdieu & Passeron, 1990; Freire, 2005). At the same time, educators are successfully transforming literacy curricula through the multiliteracies pedagogy, with the goal of increasing students' powerful participation in a multiliterate culture. Multiliteracies represents the beginning of the reflexive move toward a culturally and linguistically diverse, and multimodal English curriculum.

Yet for this to occur, inequitable school practices, which are not part of the multiliteracies pedagogy, need to change. For example, in this school, ability grouping was used to parcel out different literacies for diverse groups of students based on uneven configurations of social power. Similarly, the school behaviour modification system invoked the use of coercive power to exclude certain students from accessing pleasurable and creative literacies.

Consequently, the school both permitted and prevented access to multiple languages and discourses, and was a system of both inclusion and exclusion. Differential access to multiliteracies resulted from unintended consequences of complex relations between intentional individual activities and social structures. Although the differential distribution of multiliteracies was reproduced by the intentional activities of individuals, the actors did not intend this outcome. The distribution of multiliteracies eluded the concerted effort of the principal and the teacher to transform the system.

Teachers and students are knowledgeable and purposive agents, who are able to be reflexive in the reordering of social practices to improve access to multiliteracies. Students were able, by varying degrees, to gain, defer to others or resist access to multiliteracies, while the teacher drew upon the available structures to recursively transform existing pedagogies to generate this access.

This is important, because access to multiliteracies was not predetermined or entirely constrained by the existing institutional structures, but was mediated by the reflexive agency of Jennifer and her students. For example, Jennifer widened the students' collaborative designing to include multiple modes and specialist media.

Access to multiliteracies, like certain self-reproducing items in nature, was found to be recursive. That is to say, access to multiliteracies was not brought into being by the agency of the teacher and students, but was continually recreated by them via the structures available. Through their activities, they reproduced the conditions that made or constrained access to multiliteracies.

For example, the outcome of the students' designing of movies for their younger peers was not exclusively the result of their own actions in the classroom. Instead, these students reproduced existing conditions, such as their cultural and linguistic resources from home and school, securing their continued degree of access to multiliteracies.

This explanation of the differential access to multiliteracies gives attention to the micro-level action of individuals in the classroom, and macro-level factors among the students' homes, communities and the wider social system. Additionally, it takes into account the enabling and constraining forces, which were at times mediated by social structures in the classroom and society, and other times, by individuals who utilised these structures in positive or negative ways.

Final Word

Historically, literacy pedagogy and research has been vigorously contested. Each wave of educational theory, intended to improve literacy education, has receded to be overcome by the next. From transmissive to progressive approaches, and from functional approaches to critical literacy, each has made definitive contributions to literacy research and practice. Yet, alone, each of these pedagogies has been insufficient for all students to access literacy learning (Mills, 2005a). This is increasingly the case as unchanged pedagogies become less relevant to the authentic textual practices of the 21st century.

Multiliteracies is an innovative attempt to combine the strengths of past approaches, while addressing the need for multimodal, digital, culturally diverse and dynamic literacies for the changing times. The digitalisation of print is progressing by the year, associated with new technologies, media and modes. Globally, the clientele of schools is increasingly charactised by local diversity and global connections. The multiliteracies classroom can be a place where cultural and linguistic diversity becomes a rich resource for literacy learning, not only for marginalised groups, but for the betterment of all.

Appendix: Pragmatic Horizon Analysis

Pragmatic horizon analysis was used to support high-level coding across each of the major themes arising from the data in this research. This analytic tool, theoretically located in Habermas' (1981) pragmatic theory of meaning – the Theory of Communicative Action, was developed by Carspecken (1996) to support important high-level inferences in critical ethnography.

Pragmatic horizon analysis involves the process of articulating validity claims in horizontal (objective, subjective and normative), and vertical (foregrounded, backgrounded and intermediate) arrays to interpret the range of possible meanings of a stretch of speech (Carspecken, 1996, 2001). Table A.1 provides an example of pragmatic horizon analysis applied to a segment of verbatim data recorded during the pilot study. The raw data are presented in the first cell of the table, and the analysis follows.

On the last day of the school quarter, the teachers grouped the students into three rooms in accordance with the whole school reward system. The teacher gathered the students who had received 'red cards' for rule breaking. These students had been placed in the lowest of three levels to complete spelling worksheets in a detention room. The others viewed an animated movie and ate ice blocks.

In this example, pragmatic horizon analysis was applied to Line 14 of the primary record ('OK. Where are all the naughties? Not the naughties – the Level Ones'). Note the horizontal or pragmatic dimension, which is the three-part distinction (denoted by separate cells in the table) between objective, subjective and normative claims of the participants.

The objective validity claim in this analysis – a statement about the world that can be observed – was simply that the teacher was assembling a certain group of students to do a certain activity. This truth claim was open to multiple accesses by others through direct observation using the senses.

The normative position regarding what 'should be' was the tacit assumption that the 'naughties' had not fulfilled their moral obligation as

Table A.1 Pragmatic horizon analysis: Pilot study example

Transcript Segment: Date: 19.09'03 Time: 10:30–10:35 am
14. J: 'OK. Where are all the naughties? Not the naughties – the Level Ones'.

Possible objective claims

Quite foregrounded, quite immediate

I've come to collect the appropriate group of students to do the drill and practice workbooks.

Less foregrounded, less immediate

I'm taking the group of students identified in our school program as having the most resistant behaviour to the school rules.

Possible normative claims

Foregrounded, less immediate

The students in level one are naughty.

Less foregrounded, less immediate

The other children are good. (And) Perhaps I shouldn't have said it that way. I'll use the correct school language for referring to these students – 'Level Ones'.

Highly backgrounded, remote, taken-for-granted

There is an expectation that students must always obey the school rules and be good.

Possible subjective claims

Quite foregrounded, quite immediate

I want you to know that I'm not happy with your behaviour.

Less foregrounded, less immediate

I'm a bit worried that I just said that. I'd better correct myself.

Highly backgrounded, remote, taken-for-granted

My actions are right as a teacher in a position of authority (identity claim).

good students and therefore, should be differentiated from the others. Also, by self-correcting her statement, there was evidence that the teacher was aware of the professional expectations within the organisation to use the legitimate or normative school discourse. In both respects, there was an assumption about what was right, wrong, good or bad.

A subjective validity claim was made when the teacher modified or self-corrected her statement with the possible intent to reinstate her identity as a fair and professional teacher. This claim had the privileged and direct access of the speaker, and therefore, is inferred by the researcher and readers of this report. The subjective claim was an assertion about the teacher's inner world, feeling, intentions and state of awareness. Social research always involves subjective validity claims because all human action is tied to the subjective references of the actor. The point for the researcher is to take into account the possible tacit meanings of this ontological category at play, rather than to simply ignore it because it is not self-evident through the senses (Carspecken, 1996).

The vertical or temporal dimension of the teacher's statement was also analysed in relation to most foregrounded or immediate meanings to most highly backgrounded or remote meanings within the objective, normative and subjective aspects of the speech (Line 14; Carspecken, 1996).

Within the normative horizon, the most foregrounded assumption was that the students who were labelled the 'naughties' were inherently bad. This claim was the most immediate or self-evident normative declaration, emphasised and apparent in the linguistic content of the act.

Labelling these students also implied a less foregrounded tacit claim that the students, from whom they were distinguished, were intrinsically good.

There was also a possible or highly backgrounded appeal to the moral expectations or norms for student behaviour within the institutional context of schooling. This backgrounded claim was a distant meaning, not immediately apparent to an observer in the linguistic content of the speech act (Carspecken, 1996).

In this way, pragmatic horizon analysis can be seen to articulate validity claims of research participants in horizontal (objective, subjective and normative) and vertical (foregrounded, backgrounded and intermediate) arrays to interpret the range of possible meanings of a stretch of speech (Carspecken, 1996, 2001).

References

Anderson, G. (1989) Critical ethnography in education: Its origins, current status and new directions. *Review of Educational Research* 59 (3), 249–270.

Anstey, M. and Bull, G. (2004) *The Literacy Labyrinth* (2nd edn). Frenchs Forest, NSW: Pearson Education Australia.

Apple, M. (1986) *Teachers and Texts: A Political Economy of Class and Gender Relations in Education*. New York, NY: Routledge and Kegan Paul.

Apple, M. (1995) Education, culture, and class power: Basil Bernstein and the Neo-Marxist sociology of education. In A.R. Sadovnik (ed.) *Knowledge and Pedagogy: The Sociology of Basil Bernstein* (pp. 45–66). Norwood, NJ: Ablex.

Apple, M. (1997) The new technology: Is it part of the solution or part of the problem in education? In G.E. Hawisher and C.L. Selfe (eds) *Literacy, Technology and Society: Confronting the Issues* (pp. 160–178). Upper Saddle River, NJ: Prentice-Hall.

Apple, M. and Weis, L. (eds) (1983) *Ideology and Practice in Schooling*. Philadelphia, PA: Temple University Press.

Australian Bureau of Statistics (2003) *Census of Population and Housing: Selected Social and Housing Characteristics Australia and Statistics Local Areas, Suburb Name, Queensland*. Canberra: Australian Bureau of Statistics.

Bakhtin, M. (1982) *The Dialogical Imagination: Four Essays* (C. Emerson and M. Holquist, trans.). Austin: University of Texas Press.

Bauer, E. and Manyak, P. (2008) Creating language-rich instruction for English-language learners. *The Reading Teacher* 62 (2), 176–178.

Berg, B. (2004) *Qualitative Research Methods for the Social Sciences* (5th edn). Sydney: Pearson.

Bezemer, J. (2008) Displaying orientation in the classroom: Students' multimodal responses to teacher instructions. *Linguistics and Education* 19, 166–178.

Bishop, R. (2003) Changing power relations in education: Kaupapa Maori messages for "mainstream" education in Aotearoa/New Zealand. *Comparative Education* 39 (2), 221–238.

Bourdieu, P. (1977) *Outline of a Theory of Practice*. Cambridge: Cambridge University Press.

Bourdieu, P. and Passeron, J.C. (1990) *Reproduction in Education, Society and Culture* (2nd edn). Beverley Hills, CA: Sage.

Bourke, C., Rigby, K. and Burden, J. (2000) *Better Practice in School Attendance: Improving the School Attendance of Indigenous Students*. Canberra, ACT: Commonwealth Department of Education, Training and Youth Affairs.

Brown, A., Ash, D., Rutherford, M., Nakagawa, K., Gordon, A. and Campione, J. (1993) Distributed expertise in the classroom. In G. Salomon (ed.) *Distributed Cognitions: Psychological and Educational Considerations* (pp. 188–228). New York, NY: Cambridge University Press.

Brown, A. and Campione, J. (1994) Guided discovery in a community of learners. In K. McGilly (ed.) *Classroom Lessons: Integrating Cognitive Theory and Classroom Practice* (pp. 229–270). Cambridge: MIT Press.

Brown, R. (2005) Learning communities and the nature of teacher participation in a learning community. *Literacy Learning: The Middle Years* 13 (2), 8–15.

Bull, G. and Anstey, M. (2003a) Critical literacies and cultural studies. In G. Bull and M. Anstey (eds) *The Literacy Lexicon* (pp. 15–36). Frenchs Forest, NSW: Pearson Education Australia.

Bull, G. and Anstey, M. (eds) (2003b) *The Literacy Lexicon*. Frenchs Forest, NSW: Pearson Education Australia.

Burn, A. and Parker, D. (2003) Tiger's big plan: Multimodality and the moving image. In C. Jewitt and G. Kress (eds) *Multimodal Literacy* (pp. 56–72). New York, NY: Peter Lang.

Burnett, G. (1995) Alternatives to ability grouping: Still unanswered questions. *Eric/Cue Digest* 111. On WWW at http://www.ericdigests.org/1996-3/ability. htm. Accessed on 30.08.10.

Burnley, I.H., Murphy, P. and Fagan, R.H. (1997) *Immigration and Australian Cities*. Annandale, NSW: Federation Press.

Callow, J. (2006) Images, politics and multiliteracies: Using a visual metalanguage. *Australian Journal of Language and Literacy* 29 (1), 7–23.

Carspecken, P. (1996) *Critical Ethnography in Educational Research: A Theoretical and Practical Guide*. New York, NY: Routledge.

Carspecken, P. (2001) Critical ethnographies from Houston: Distinctive features and directions. In P. Carspecken and G. Walford (eds) *Critical Ethnography and Education* (Vol. 5, pp. 1–26). Oxford: Elsevier Science.

Cazden, C. (1988) *Classroom Discourse: The Language of Teaching and Learning*. Portsmouth, NH: Heinemann.

Cazden, C. (1992) *Whole Language Plus: Essays on Literacy in the United States and New Zealand*. New York, NY: Teachers College Press.

Cook-Gumperz, J. (ed.) (1986) *The Social Construction of Literacy: Studies in Interactional Socio-Linguistics* (Vol. 3). Cambridge: Cambridge University Press.

Cope, B. and Kalantzis, M. (1997) Multiliteracies, education and the new communications environment: A response to Vaughan Prain. *Discourse: Studies in the Cultural Politics of Education* 18 (3), 469–478.

Cope, B. and Kalantzis, M. (1999) Teaching and learning in the new world of literacy: A professional development program and classroom research project: Participants' Resource Book. Melbourne: RMIT University, Faculty of Education, Language and Community Services.

Cope, B. and Kalantzis, M. (2000a) Designs for social futures. In B. Cope and M. Kalantzis (eds) *Multiliteracies: Literacy Learning and the Design of Social Futures* (pp. 203–234). South Yarra, VIC: Macmillan.

Cope, B. and Kalantzis, M. (2000b) Introduction: Multiliteracies: The beginnings of an idea. In B. Cope and M. Kalantzis (eds) *Multiliteracies: Literacy Learning and the Design of Social Futures* (pp. 3–8). South Yarra, VIC: Macmillan.

Cope, B. and Kalantzis, M. (2000c) *Multiliteracies: Literacy Learning and the Design of Social Futures*. South Yarra, VIC: Macmillan.

Delpit, L. (1988) The silenced dialogue: Power and pedagogy in educating other people's children. *Harvard Educational Review* 5 (3), 280–298.

Dewey, J. (1966) *Democracy and Education*. New York, NY: Free Press.

Fairclough, N. (2000) Multiliteracies and language: Orders of discourse and inter-textuality. In B. Cope and M. Kalantzis (eds) *Multiliteracies: Literacy Learning and the Design of Social Futures* (pp. 162–181). South Yarra, VIC: Macmillan.

Farkas, G. (1996) *Human Capital or Cultural Capital? Ethnicity and Poverty Groups in an Urban School District*. Hawthorne, NY: Aldine de Gruyter.

Foucault, M. (1977) *Discipline and Punish: The Birth of the Prison* (A. Sheridan, trans.). London: Penguin Books.

Freire, P. (2005) *Education for Critical Consciousness*. London: Continuum.

Freire, P. and Macedo, D. (1987) *Literacy: Reading the Word and the World*. Hadley, MA: Bergin and Garvey.

Gaver, W.W. (1991) Technology affordances. Paper presented at the SIGCHI Conference on Human Factors in Computing Systems: Reaching through technology, New Orleans, Louisiana.

Gee, J. (1992) *The Social Mind: Language, Ideology, and Social Practice*. New York, NY: Bergin and Garvey.

Gee, J. (1993) *An Introduction to Human Language: Fundamental Concepts*. Englewood Cliffs, NJ: Prentice-Hall.

Gee, J. (1994) New alignments and old literacies: From fast capitalism to the canon. Paper presented at the 1994 Australian Reading Association Twentieth National Conference. Carlton South, Victoria: Australian Reading Association, pp. 1–35.

Gee, J. (1996) *Social Linguistics and Literacies: Ideology in Discourses* (2nd edn). New York, NY: Routledge and Falmer.

Gee, J. (2000) New people in new worlds: Networks, the new capitalism and schools. In B. Cope and M. Kalantzis (eds) *Multiliteracies: Literacy Learning and the Design of Social Futures* (pp. 43–68). South Yarra: Macmillan.

Gee, J. (2003) *What Video Games have to Teach us about Learning and Literacy*. New York, NY: Palgrave, Macmillan.

Giddens, A. (1979) *Central Problems in Social Theory*. London: Macmillan.

Giddens, A. (1981) Agency, institution, and time-space analysis. In K. Knorr-Cetina and A. Cicourel (eds) *Advances in Social Theory and Methodology: Toward an Integration of Micro and Macro Sociology* (pp. 161–174). Boston, MA: Routledge and Kegan Paul.

Giddens, A. (1984) *The Constitution of Society: Outline of a Theory of Structuration*. Cambridge: Polity Press.

Giroux, H. (1988) *Schooling and the Struggle for Public Life: Critical Pedagogy in the Modern Age*. Minneapolis: University of Minnesota Press.

Giroux, H.A. (1990) Critical theory and the politics of culture and voice: Rethinking the discourse of educational research. In R.R. Sherman and R.B. Webb (eds) *Qualitative Research in Education: Focus and Methods* (pp. 190–210). East Sussex: The Falmer Press.

Gittins, R. and Tiffen, R. (2004) *How Australia Compares*. Port Melbourne, Australia: Cambridge University Press.

Goldenberg, C. (1992) Instructional conversations: Promoting comprehension through discussion. *The Reading Teacher* 46 (4), 316–326.

Goldenberg, C. and Patthey-Chavez, G. (1995) Discourse processes in instructional conversations: Interactions between teacher and transition readers. *Discourse Processes* 19 (1), 57–74.

Gore, J.M. (1988) Disciplining bodies: On the continuity of power relations in pedagogy. In J.M. Gore (ed.) *Foucault's Challenge: Discourse, Knowledge and Power in Education* (pp. 231–254). New York, NY: Teachers College Columbia University.

Grenfell, M. (2004) Bourdieu in the classroom. In M. Olssen (ed.) *Culture and Learning: Access and Opportunity in the Classroom* (pp. 49–72). London: Information Age Publishing.

Habermas, J. (1981) *The Theory of Communicative Action: Reason and the Rationalisation of Society* (Vol. 1). Boston, MA: Beacon Press.

Hamston, J. (2006) Pathways to multiliteracies: Student teachers' critical reflections on a multimodal text. *The Australian Journal of Language and Literacy* 29 (1), 38–51.

Heath, S. (1983) *Ways with Words: Language, Life and Work in Communities and Classrooms*. Cambridge: Cambridge University Press.

Heath, S. (1999) Literacy and social practice. In D. Wagner, R. Venezky and B. Street (eds) *Literacy: An International Handbook* (pp. 102–106). Boulder, CO: Westview Press.

Heron, J. and Reason, P. (2001) The practice of co-operative inquiry: Research 'with' rather than 'on' people. In P. Reason and H. Bradbury (eds) *Handbook of Action Research: Participative Inquiry and Practice* (pp. 179–188). Thousand Oaks, CA: Sage.

Holland, D.C., Lachicotte, W., Skinner, D. and Cain, C. (1998) *Identity and Agency in Cultural Worlds*. Cambridge, MA: Harvard University Press.

Hull, G. and Nelson, M. (2005) Locating the semiotic power of multimodality. *Written Communication* 22 (2), 224–261.

Jenkins, R. (1992) *Pierre Bourdieu*. London: Routledge.

Jewitt, C. (2006) *Technology, Literacy and Learning: A Multimodal Approach*. Abingdon, Oxon: Routledge.

Jewitt, C. and Kress, G. (2003) *Multimodal Literacy*. New York, NY: Peter Lang Publishing.

Kalantzis, M. and Cope, B. (2000a) A multiliteracies pedagogy: A pedagogical supplement. In B. Cope and M. Kalantzis (eds) *Multiliteracies: Literacy Learning and the Design of Social Futures* (pp. 239–248). South Yarra, VIC: Macmillan.

Kalantzis, M. and Cope, B. (2000b) Changing the role of schools. In B. Cope and M. Kalantzis (eds) *Multiliteracies: Literacy Learning and the Design of Social Futures* (pp. 121–148). South Yarra: Macmillan.

Kalantzis, M. and Cope, B. (eds) (2005) *Learning by Design*. Melbourne, VIC: Victorian Schools Innovation Commission and Common Ground.

Kalantzis, M. and Cope, B. (2008) *New Learning: Elements of a Science of Education*. Port Melbourne, VIC: Cambridge University Press.

Kalantzis, M., Cope, B. and Fehring, H. (2002) Multiliteracies: Teaching and learning in the new communications environment. *Primary English Notes* 133, 1–8.

Kaspersen, L.B. (2000) *Anthony Giddens: An Introduction to a Social Theorist* (S. Sampson, trans.). Oxford: Blackwell Publishers.

Khattri, N., Riley, K. and Kane, M. (1997) Students at risk in poor rural areas: A review of research. *Journal of Research in Rural Education* 13 (2), 79–100.

Kipp, M. (2005) *Gesture Generation by Imitation: From Human Behaviour to Computer Character Animation*. Boca Raton, FL: Universal Publishers.

Kress, G. (1993) Language as social practice. In G. Kress (ed.) *Communication and Culture* (pp. 71–130). Kensington, NSW: New South Wales University Press.

Kress, G. (2000a) Design and transformation: New theories of meaning. In B. Cope and M. Kalantzis (eds) *Multiliteracies: Literacy Learning and the Design of Social Futures* (pp. 153–161). South Yarra, VIC: Macmillan.

Kress, G. (2000b) Multimodality. In B. Cope and M. Kalantzis (eds) *Multiliteracies: Literacy Learning and the Design of Social Futures* (pp. 182–202). South Yarra, VIC: Macmillan.

Kress, G. and van Leeuwen, T. (1996) *Reading Images: The Grammar of Visual Design*. London: Routledge.

Kress, G., Jewitt, C., Ogborn, J. and Tsatsarelis, C. (2001) *Multimodal Teaching and Learning: The Rhetorics of the Science Classroom*. London: Continuum.

Labov, W. (1972) *Sociolinguistic Patterns*. Philadelphia, PA: University of Pennsylvania Press.

Lather, P. (1990) Reinscribing otherwise: The play of values in the practice of human science. In E. Guba (ed.) *The Paradigm Dialog* (pp. 315–355). Newbury Park: Sage.

Lather, P. (1991) *Getting Smart: Feminist Research and Pedagogy within the Postmodern*. New York, NY: Routledge.

Lave, J. (1988) *Cognition in Practice: Mind, Mathematics, and Culture in Everyday Life*. Cambridge: Cambridge University Press.

Lave, J. and Wenger, E. (eds) (1991) *Situated Learning: Legitimate Peripheral Participation*. Cambridge: Cambridge University Press.

Leander, K.M. (2002) Locating Latanya: The situated production of identity artifacts in classroom interaction. *Research in the Teaching of English* 37, 198–250.

LeCompte, M., Millroy, W. and Preissle, J. (1992) *The Handbook of Qualitative Research in Education*. San Diego, CA: Academic Press.

Lefebvre, H. (1991) *The Production of Space* (D. Nicholson-Smith, trans.). London: Blackwell.

Lo Bianco, J. (2000) Multiliteracies and multilingualism. In B. Cope and M. Kalantzis (eds) *Multiliteracies: Literacy Learning and the Design of Social Futures* (pp. 92–105). South Yarra, VIC: Macmillan.

Luke, A. (1988) *Literacy, Textbooks and Ideology*. London: Falmer Press.

Luke, A. and Freebody, P. (1997) Shaping the social practices of reading. In S. Muspratt, A. Luke and P. Freebody (eds) *Constructing Critical Literacies: Teaching and Learning Textual Practice* (pp. 185–225). Sydney: Allen & Unwin.

Luke, A. and Freebody, P. (1999) A map of possible practices: Further notes on the four resources model. *Practically Primary* 4 (2), 5–8.

Luke, A., Comber, B. and Grant, H. (2003) Critical literacies and cultural studies. In M. Anstey and G. Bull (eds) *The Literacy Lexicon* (2nd edn, pp. 15–35). Frenchs Forest, NSW: Pearson Education Australia.

Martin-Jones, M. and Saxena, M. (1996) Turn-taking, power asymmetries, and the positioning of bilingual participants in classroom discourse. *Linguistics and Education* 8, 105–123.

Maxwell, J. (2005) *Qualitative Research Design: An Interactive Approach*. Thousand Oaks, CA: Sage Publications.

MCEECDYA (2009) National Assessment Program Literacy and Numeracy. On WWW at http://www.naplan.edu.au/home_page.html. Accessed on 07.01.10.

McLaren, P. (1993) *Schooling as Ritual Performance: Towards a Political Economy of Educational Symbols and Gestures* (2nd edn). London: Routledge.

McLaren, P. (1994) *Life in Schools: An Introduction to Critical Pedagogy in the Foundations of Education* (2nd edn). White Plains, NY: Longman.

McLaren, P. and Leonard, P. (eds) (1993) *Paulo Freire: A Critical Encounter* (2nd edn). London: Routledge.

McNeil, D. (1992) *Hand and Mind: What Gestures Reveal about Thought*. London: The University of Chicago Press.

Mehan, H. (1979) *Learning Lessons*. Cambridge, MA: Harvard University Press.

Mills, K.A. (2005a) Deconstructing binary oppositions in literacy discourse and pedagogy. *Australian Journal of Language and Literacy* 28 (1), 67–82.

Mills, K.A. (2005b) Multiliteracies: Remnant discourses and pedagogies. Paper presented at the Australian Literacy Educator's Association/Australian Association of the Teaching of English National Conference 2005: Pleasure, Passion, Provocation, Broadbeach.

Mills, K.A. (2006a) Discovering design possibilities through a pedagogy of multiliteracies. *Journal of Learning Design* 1 (3), 61–72.

Mills, K.A. (2006b) Mr. Travelling-at-will Ted Doyle: Discourses in a multiliteracies classroom. *Australian Journal of Language and Literacy* 28 (2), 132–149.

Mills, K.A. (2006c) Multiliteracies: A critical ethnography: Pedagogy, power, discourse and access to multiliteracies. Unpublished PhD thesis, Queensland University of Technology, Brisbane.

Mills, K.A. (2006d) We've been wastin' a whole million watchin' her doin' her shoes: Situated practice within a pedagogy of multiliteracies. *The Australian Educational Researcher* 33 (3), 13–34.

Mills, K.A. (2007) Have you seen Lord of the Rings? Power, pedagogy and discourses in a multiliteracies classroom. *Journal of Language, Identity, and Education* 6 (3), 221–241.

Mills, K.A. (2008a) Multiliteracies and a new metalanguage for the moving image. Paper presented at the AARE Changing Climates: Education for Sustainable Futures: 30th November–4th December, Brisbane.

Mills, K.A. (2008b) Transformed practice in a pedagogy of multiliteracies. *Pedagogies: An International Journal* 3 (2), 109–128.

Mills, K.A. (2009) Multiliteracies: Interrogating competing discourses. *Language and Education* 23 (2), 103–116.

Mills, K.A. (2010a) Filming in progress: New spaces for multimodal designing. *Linguistics and Education* 21, 14–28.

Mills, K.A. (2010b) A review of the 'Digital Turn'. *New Literacy Studies, Review of Educational Research* 80 (2), 246–271.

Mills, K.A. (2010c) Shrek meets Vygotsky: Rethinking adolescents multimodal literacy practices in schools. *Journal of Adolescent and Adult Literacy* 54 (1), 35–45.

Morgan, W., Russell, A. and Ryan, M. (2002) Informed opportunism: Teaching for learning in uncertain contexts of distributed education. In M. Lea and K. Nicolls (eds) *Distributed Learning* (pp. 38–55). London: Routledge Falmer.

Nakata, M. (2000) History, cultural diversity and English language teaching. In B. Cope and M. Kalantzis (eds) *Multiliteracies: Literacy Learning and the Design of Social Futures* (pp. 106–120). South Yarra, VIC: Macmillan.

Nelson, M.E. (2006) Mode, meaning and synaesthesia in multimedia L2 writing. *Language Learning and Technology* 10 (2), 56–76.

New London Group (1996) A pedagogy of multiliteracies: Designing social futures. *Harvard Educational Review* 66 (1), 60–92.

New London Group (2000) A pedagogy of multiliteracies: Designing social futures. In B. Cope and M. Kalantzis (eds) *Multiliteracies: Literacy Learning and the Design of Social Futures* (pp. 9–38). South Yarra, VIC: Macmillan.

Nordlund, C. (2006) Art experiences in Waldorf Education: Graduates' meaning making reflections. University of Missouri Columbia.

Oakes, J. (1990) *Multiplying Inequalities: The Effects of Race, Class, and Tracking on Opportunities to Learn Math and Science*. Santa Monica: RAND.

Osbourne, B. and Wilson, E. (2003) Multiliteracies in the Torres Strait: A Mabuiag Island State School diabetes project. *Australian Journal of Language and Literacy* 26 (1), 23–38.

Popkewitz, T. and Guba, E. (1990) *Whose Future? Whose Past? Notes on Critical Theory and Methodology*. Newbury Park: Sage.

Quantz, R. (1992) On critical ethnography (with some postmodern considerations). In M. LeCompte, W. Millroy and W. Preissle (eds) *The Handbook of Qualitative Research in Education* (pp. 447–505). San Diego, CA: Academic Press.

Queensland Studies Authority (2007a) National assessment program – literacy and numeracy. On WWW at http://www.qsa.qld.edu.au/testing/357tests/news.html. Accessed on 29.12.07.

Queensland Studies Authority (2007b) *Queensland Year 3, 5 and 7 Tests in Aspects of Literacy and Numeracy*. Brisbane: Queensland Government.

Reece, J. (1976) *Lester and Clyde*. Sydney, NSW: Scholastic.

Rolfe, M. (1998) Suburbia. In P. Bell and R.J. Bell (eds) *Americanization and Australia* (pp. 61–80). Sydney: UNSW Press.

Ryan, C. and Watson, L. (2005) The drift to private schools in Australia: Understanding its features. From Australian National University. On WWW at http://www.hdl.handle.net/1885/42681. Accessed on 17.01.10.

Siegel, M. (1995) More than words: The generative power of transmediation for learning. *Canadian Journal of Education* 20 (4), 455–475.

Soja, E.W. (1980) The socio-spatial dialectic. *Annals of the Association of America Geographers* 70 (2), 207–225.

Soja, E.W. (1989) *Postmodern Geographies: The Reassertion of Space in Critical Social Theory*. Oxford: Verso.

Stein, P. (2006) The Olifantsvlei fresh stories project: Multimodality, creativity, and fixing in the semiotic chain. In C. Jewitt and G. Kress (eds) *Multimodal Literacy* (pp. 123–138). New York, NY: Peter Lang.

Stein, P. (2007) *Multimodal Pedagogies in Diverse Classrooms: Representation, Rights, and Resources*. Abingdon: Routledge.

Street, B. (ed.) (1993) *Cross Cultural Approaches to Literacy*. Cambridge: Cambridge University Press.

Street, B. (1995) *Social Literacies: Critical Approaches to Literacy in Development, Ethnography and Education*. London: Longman.

Stuebing, S., Celsi, J. and Cousineau, L.K. (1994) *Environments that Support New Modes of Learning: The Results of Two Interactive Design Workshops*. Cupertino, CA: Apple Computer.

Suhor, C. (1984) Towards a semiotic-based curriculum. *Journal of Curriculum Studies* 16 (3), 247–257.

Thesen, L. (2001) Modes, literacy and power: A university case study. *Language and Education* 15 (2), 132–145.

Unsworth, L. (2006) Multiliteracies and a metalanguage of image/text relations: Implications for teaching English as a first or additional language in the 21st century. *TESOL in Context, Series S: Special Edition* 1, 147–162.

Valk, F.V. (2008) Identity power and representation in virtual environments. *Journal of Online Learning and Teaching* 4 (2), 201–211.

van Eck, R. (2006) Digital game-based learning: It's not just the digital natives who are restless. *Educause Review* 41 (2), 16–30.

Vygotsky, L. (1962) *Thought and Language.* Cambridge, MA: Massachusetts Institute of Technology.

Vygotsky, L. (1978) *Mind in Society: The Development of Higher Psychological Processes.* London: Harvard University Press.

Willis, P. (1977) *Learning to Labour: How Working Class Kids get Working Class Jobs.* Hampshire: Gower Publishing Company.

Index